JUSTIN SCROGGIE

Tic Tac Teddy Bears & Teardrop Tattoos

First published in Great Britain in 2008 by Hodder & Stoughton

An Hachette Livre UK company

1

Copyright © Justin Scroggie 2008

The right of Justin Scroggie to be identified as the Author of the Work has been asserted by him in accordance with the Copyright, Designs and Patents Act 1988.

A CIP catalogue record for this title is available from the British Library

ISBN 978 0340 976487

Designed and typeset in Stempel Garamond and P22 Underground by Estuary English

Printed and bound by Mackays of Chatham Ltd, Chatham, Kent

Hodder & Stoughton policy is to use papers that are natural, renewable and recyclable products and made from wood grown in sustainable forests. The logging and manufacturing processes are expected to conform to the environmental regulations of the country of origin.

Hodder & Stoughton Ltd
338 Euston Road
London NW1 3BH

www.hodder.co.uk

JUSTIN SCROGGIE

A MISCELLANY OF THE SIGNS AND SYMBOLS YOU SEE EVERY DAY

HODDER &
STOUGHTON

CONTENTS

INTRODUCTION 7

1. MEETING 8

2. ACCESSORIES 20

3. ON THE BODY 29

4. IN CLOTHES 36

5. IN WARTIME 40

6. ON THE STREET 47

7. DOWN THE PUB 56

8. THE NAME OF THE ROAD 60

9. IN THE LAYOUT 62

10. IN THE SHAPE OF THE BUILDING 65

11. ON A BUILDING 68

12. SECRET BUILDINGS 75

13. IN ESPIONAGE 79

14. AT A CARD GAME 87

15. IN SPORT 90

16. IN A NUMBER 101

17. AT THE MOVIES 107

18. ON TELEVISION 113

19. IN ART 119

20. IN THE MONEY 125

21. IN THE POST 130

22. IN LITERATURE 134

23. IN A DIARY 138

24. IN THE BIBLE 141

25. IN CHURCH 144

26. AT A CHURCH WEDDING 152

27. IN A CHURCHYARD 156

28. IN THE GARDEN 161

29. IN THE COUNTRY 168

30. AT THE PALACE 176

31. IN A COAT OF ARMS 180

32. IN MUSIC 182

33. OVERHEARD 193

34. ON A COMPUTER OR MOBILE 197

35. IN THE PAPER 202

36. ON A CAR 214

37. ON A MOTORBIKE 230

38. ON A LORRY 233

39. IN AN EMERGENCY 236

40. IN HOSPITAL 240

41. IN FOOD & DRINK 245

42. AT THE BINGO 251

43. IN PARLIAMENT 253

ACKNOWLEDGEMENTS 255

INTRODUCTION

If there is a door marked 'Private' I want to know what's behind it. If I see a squiggle on a wall, I wonder what it means. If I hear a conversation between people in-the-know, I want to understand what they are saying.

This book is about pushing open those doors. And there are hundreds and hundreds of private doors, secret symbols, covert conversations all around us, all the time. Spoken language is only one of the many ways human beings talk to each other. And let's face it, there's nothing more irritating than friends who chat in a foreign language you don't understand, whether they're talking Russian, football or computers.

So why is that Tic-Tac man at the racecourse waving his white-gloved hands about? What is he saying, and why doesn't he want me to know what it is? That hairy scary bloke's got a teddy bear, what does that mean? Why do some people in prison have a teardrop tattooed under their eye?

Be nosy. Find out. Read the book.

1. MEETING

KU KLUX KLAN

Klansmen use the acronym KIGY ('Klansman I Greet You') as a secret greeting, and in email and web addresses. In conversation a member might say AYAK ('Are you a Klansman?') to identify himself. The response is AKIA ('A Klansman I am').

The KKK arose after the American Civil War with an agenda of white supremacy in response to Republican policies of reconstruction. In their white flowing robes, with their horses' hooves muffled, the Klansmen posed as the ghosts of Confederate soldiers returning to save the nation.

The second KKK flourished after WW1 adding anti-Semitism and anti-Catholicism to its belief system. The civil-rights movement of

the 1960s gave the Klan new impetus, with attacks against blacks and civil-rights workers throughout the South.

Just after WW2 Superman took on the KKK on the radio, using real Klan code words supplied by author Stetson Kennedy, who infiltrated the Klan. It's a long way from Smallville.

(*See also:* 16: **IN A NUMBER;** 32. **IN MUSIC,** *Band Names*)

MYTH ALERT

Have you heard the urban legend that:
- Cigarette brand Marlboro is owned by the Klan
- According to urban legend, if you lay a pack on its side, the red chevrons on three sides make 3 'K's
- The 'Veni, Vidi, Vici' motto is the motto of the Klan
- If you turn the pack upside down, 'Marlboro' reads 'orobl jeW', an anti-Semitic message.

The Marlboro brand is actually part of the publicly owned Philip Morris Company, and was named after Marlborough Street in London where the company factory was based. 'Veni, Vidi, Vici' is a quotation by Julius Caesar in 47 BC: 'I came, I saw, I conquered'.

Rich and powerful corporations attract conspiracy theories (similarly the Coca Cola script on its side is said to show a man snorting cocaine), and cigarette packs seem to attract the strangest myths; for example, the camel on a Camel cigarette pack has a man with an erection hidden in the artwork (look at the front left leg). And there is a story, still going round schools, that Lucky Strikes are 'lucky' because 1 in a 100 cigarettes contains pot.

(*See also* 36. **ON A CAR,** *Myth Alert*)

FREEMASONS

Freemasonry has many 'secret' signs used in plain view, among them the hammer, and the set square and compasses.

One of the most often mentioned is the handshake, by which one Brother lets

another know that he is in the Brotherhood. It's like a normal handshake, right hand to right, except that the thumb is pressed into a knuckle of the other man's finger. The handshake varies from lodge to lodge but essentially, the knuckles represent the first three Craft 'degrees' or levels of Masonic membership:

- **1ST DEGREE** 'Entered Apprentice', the degree of an Initiate. Press your thumb on the other man's index finger knuckle

- **2ND DEGREE** 'Fellow Craft'. Press your thumb on the other man's middle finger knuckle

- **3RD DEGREE** 'Master Mason'. Press your thumb on the other man's third finger knuckle

The Mason's shake is a curiously intimate gesture, and once you get the hang of it, you may remember times when you were gently sounded out without realising.

(*See also* **9. IN THE LAYOUT**, *Washington DC*)

THE FAR RIGHT

Extreme right-wing groups love acronyms. The neo-Nazi gang in *American History X* (1998) call themselves the 'Disciples of Christ' or DOC – real neo-Nazis use the DOC tattoo in homage – even though the movie is about a racist who sees the error of his ways.

Acronyms are also used as tags for slogans, websites, email addresses and online greetings:

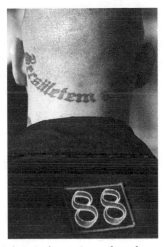

- **ORION** Our Race is Our Nation
- **WPWW** White Pride World Wide
- **ROA** Race Over All
- **UAO** United as One
- **RAHOWA** Racial Holy War
- **CI** Christian Identity
- **SWP** Supreme White Power

Numbers carry great significance among far-right groups. They are usually based on a substitution code, where 1 equals A, 2 equals B, etc. The trick is in knowing what the letters stand for.

For example, 18 stands for 'AH', Adolf Hitler, from which the group Combat 18 took their name. 88 stands for 'Heil Hitler'. 28 stands for 'BH' – 'Blood and Honour' – an extreme right-wing group that organises white-power concerts. Blood and Honour (Blut und Ehre) was the motto of Hitler Youth.

(*See also* 16. **IN A NUMBER**; 4. **IN CLOTHES**, *Red Shoelaces* and *Lonsdale*)

FRIEND OF DOROTHY

The phrase 'Friend of Dorothy?' was a secret sign when homosexuality was still illegal in the UK and USA. Using it in conversation allowed a gay man to ask another man if he was gay, without giving too much away.

It probably comes from *The Wizard of Oz* (1939), in which Dorothy Gale accepts people who are different: the Tin Man, Scarecrow, and the Cowardly Lion without a 'noive' who lives a lie:

'I'm afraid there's no denyin', I'm just a dandy lion.'

Dorothy is a gay icon, as by association is Judy Garland. Another possible origin of the phrase is American wit Dorothy Parker, famous for her gay male friends.

According to the late journalist Randy Shilts, the use of the phrase among the gay military triggered an investigation by the Naval Investigative Service (now the NCIS of TV fame) in 1981, as they hunted for a 'mastermind' at the centre of a ring of homosexual personnel – a mysterious woman called Dorothy!

You don't hear the phrase so much these days, though you might, for example, see codified adverts for 'FOD meetings' among the daily events on a cruise ship. Since the outing of Hogwarts' headmaster in 2007 by Harry Potter author J.K. Rowling, another wizardly fable has spawned a phrase for the gay and lesbian population: D.A. or Dumbledore's Army.

TEDDY BEARS

If you see a large hairy man growl and say 'Woof!' to another similar fellow, he may be signalling that he is a 'Bear'.

Bears are hairy, chubby homosexual men who reject the stereotype

of the slim, smooth-skinned good-looking gay guy or the camp queen. The image of the Bear is masculine, protective and loyal – gruff and grizzly on the outside but warm and fuzzy on the inside.

In the 1970s the 'Bear' version of the handkerchief code was to carry a small teddy bear in your back pocket. Today it is more common to see a paw-print tattoo, or the 'Bear' flag: a sepia-toned version of the rainbow flag, with a paw-print top left. This symbol appears on key fobs, lapel pins, necklaces and yes, even teddy bears.

(*See also* 4. **IN CLOTHES**, *Handkerchief Code*)

MILITARY SALUTES

Not sure if a military type is in the Navy or the Army? Watch their salute. In the Army, the palm faces outwards. In the Navy the palm faces downwards. The Navy salute probably derives from 'tipping your hat'.

According to another theory, Queen Victoria was saluted while inspecting a ship and was appalled by the ratings' hands, dirty and blistered from swabbing the deck. Since then the Navy 'hide' their hands when saluting.

Saluting evolved in the Middle Ages. When two armoured knights met on horseback, they raised their visors with their right hand, showing their face and indicating that their hand carried no weapon.

Similarly, at the command 'All hands on deck', naval personnel show themselves on deck and visibly grasp the rigging (nowadays the guard-rail), signalling that the guns are unmanned and no small arms are carried.

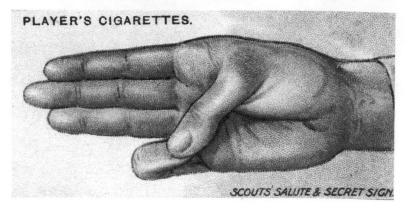

PLAYER'S CIGARETTES.

SCOUTS SALUTE & SECRET SIGN.

SCOUTS

Scouts across the world greet each other using a left-handed handshake. In 1890 Baden-Powell entered Kumasi, capital city of the Ashanti. He was met by a Great Chief and held out his right hand in greeting. The Chief, however, transferred the shield in his left hand to his right, and used his (now free) left hand to return the handshake. This was a sign of trust and friendship, he explained, because with no shield, a warrior is open to attack. Baden-Powell adopted this 'friendship' handshake for his Scout Movement.

Scouts also have a secret sign. Hold up your right hand to your shoulder, palm outwards, thumb resting on the nail of your little finger, the other three fingers pointing upwards. The three fingers remind the Scout of his three promises: to honour God and the monarch, help others and obey Scout Law. The same hand position is raised to the forehead for a full salute.

Unlike the Scouts, the Boys' Brigade members shake with their right hand. But they keep the little finger separate and interlock it with the other person's little finger. The BB badge is an anchor, a Christian symbol of hope and faithfulness.

(*See also* 13. **IN ESPIONAGE**, *Baden-Powell*; 29. **IN THE COUNTRY**, *Trail Signs*)

BLOODS AND CRIPS

Crip hand sign

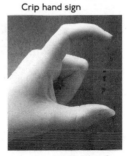

The Bloods and the Crips are two notorious and rival street gangs based in Los Angeles whose hand signs, clothing, greetings and graffiti have done much to influence young British culture.

Many of the gang signs you may see in Britain are just kids imitating 'cool' references; it doesn't necessarily mean they are Crips or Bloods, any more than taping *The Sopranos* means you're in the Mafia.

■ **CRIPS** The Crips originated in 1969. Their signs and symbols include:

- Colour blue (also grey, orange and purple)
- Colours usually worn to the right – bandanna hanging from right pocket, hats tilted right, blue laces in right shoe, right sleeve or trouser leg rolled up, right eyebrow shaved, etc.
- Call each other 'Cuzz' and themselves BK or 'Blood Killas'
- Call the Bloods 'Slobs' as disrespect
- Use letter 'C' instead of 'B' or crossing out letter 'B' to disrespect Bloods
- British Knight (BK) trainers
- A tattoo is the three-point crown

The 'Crip Walk' is a series of dance-like foot movements that spell out Crip-related words, or spell out rival gang words and then erase them as an insult. The Walk entered the mainstream via hip-hop, e.g. Rappers WC and Snoop Dogg.

■ **BLOODS** The Bloods originated in 1971. Their signs and symbols include:

- Colour red (also black, brown and pink)

- Colours usually worn to the left
  – bandanna hanging from left pocket,
  hats tilted left, red laces in left shoe,
  left sleeve or trouser leg rolled up, left
  eyebrow shaved etc.

- Calling each other 'Blood'

- Using the word 'Piru'

- CK for 'Crip Killas' in hand signs and graffiti

Blood 'Crip Killa'
hand sign

- Calvin Klein (CK) clothing

- Letter 'C' crossed out to disrespect Crips

- Hand signs that spell the word 'blood'

- Dog paw symbol of three dots, as tattoo or burn

- The acronym MOB for Member of Blood

HAND SIGNS

Hand signs are 'thrown' as non-verbal signals between gang
members, and to diss members of rival gangs.

LEAGUE OF OVALTINEYS

Remember the 'Ovaltineys'? Nor do I. However, in 1939 over five
million British children were enrolled in the League – more than 10
per cent of the population!

In the 1930s The League of Ovaltineys were a group of children
who advertised Ovaltine, a malty drink from Switzerland originally
designed as a vitamin booster for invalids. Their jingle was so
popular they had their own show on Radio Luxembourg.

Their secret sign was to hold up their right hand, palm outwards,
using their thumb and forefinger to make an 'O'. To reply, you held
up your hand making a 'V' with your thumb and forefinger, the
other three fingers being closed.

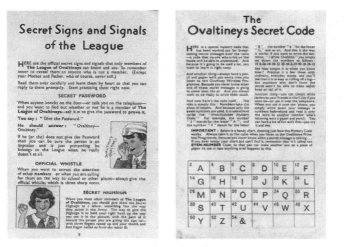

Right forefinger to the right side of your nose meant: 'Come over to my house after school.' Left forefinger to the left side of your nose: 'Watch out, someone's trying to discover our secrets.' Tapping your Ovaltiney badge three times with your right forefinger: 'Let's go home.'

The secret signal was three sharp notes, and the password 'Ovaltiney, Ovaltiney'. There was also a 'mystery code', basically an alpha-numeric substitution code using even numbers only.

STRANGE FACT

Ovaltine was the official drink of the 1948 Olympics!

KISSING

From theatrical air kisses to Madonna and Britney's full-on snog at the MTV awards, a kiss is rarely just a kiss.

We've all printed an 'X' on a card or an email to represent a kiss. In the past illiterate people would sign a document by

marking it with an X and then kissing the X as a sign of sincerity – literally 'sealed with a kiss'.

In ancient Rome, a public 'basium' or lip-to-lip kiss before witnesses sealed a couple's marriage and probably became the origin of our 'kiss the bride' tradition at the end of a church wedding.

Early Christians greeted each other with a 'holy kiss', to transfer the 'spirit' from one to the other. Holy kissing was forbidden on Maundy Thursday because of the 'Judas Kiss'. In the gospels (Matthew 26:47-50, Mark 14:44-45) Judas Iscariot kisses Jesus as a secret sign that Jesus was the man to arrest and so betrays Him. This was no chaste peck. Both Matthew and Mark use the Greek *kataphilein*, meaning 'to kiss firmly, passionately, tenderly or warmly'.

Crusaders raised their sword and kissed the cross-section before going into battle. This may be the origin of the 'recover' position in the modern Navy.

The Judas Kiss was echoed in *The Godfather Part II* (1974), when Michael Corleone kisses Fredo passionately, signifying that it was Fredo who went against the Family.

CONTINENTAL KISSES

Who, how, and how many times, should you kiss? There is no definitive answer, so please treat the following as a rough guide at best.

Women kiss each other, as do men and women. Men kiss men only if they are good friends or family. When you kiss, keep your hands to your sides. Don't hold an arm or a waist. This helps to create suitable distance. And remember it isn't an invitation to snog; kissing the air behind the other person's ear is fine.

How many? It varies across Europe and from region to region. In Italy and Germany, kissing is generally restricted to close friends and family.

Nicolas Sarkhozy meets and greets

In Belgium, once is enough. In Paris and central France, one on each cheek is the norm, right cheek first. Also in Spain, Austria and Scandinavia. In the Netherlands, three kisses are the best bet, starting and ending on the right cheek. In Brittany, you kiss like this when you arrive, but add a fourth kiss when you leave. In northern France it can be four from the start.

VW CAMPERS

Every summer, a fleet of ageing Volkswagen dormobiles sets off across Europe with Australians or Kiwis at the helm. When the vans pass each other, they make the surfers' 'Shaka' sign.

Just close your three middle fingers, and stick out your thumb and little finger. The 'W' silhouette represents the VW logo.

Just be careful where you use the sign: in some countries it symbolises a bong, and indicates the use of marijuana.

2. ACCESSORIES

ANKLETS

Not all anklet wearers are swingers! But it is worth taking a discreet look at anklet design, as it may indicate a swinger.

Swingers are couples who enjoy having sex with other singles or couples. As with other alternative lifestyles, some swingers use secret symbols to recognise each other.

⚥	MFFM sign: Male, Female, Female, Male combination
HW	Hot Wife
⚥	Male, Female, Male combination
⚥	Female, Male, Female combination
MILF	Mother I'd like to F**k
IR	Inter-racial
♠	Queen of **SPADES**: White woman with a sexual preference for black men

These signs may also be displayed as necklaces, tattoos or dog-tags.

 The male/female symbols have engendered the transgender symbol. It includes the two 'arms', with a third that combines both in one arm. NB: it is a symbol of gender and identity and is not used by swingers.

(*See also* 3. **ON THE BODY**, *Tattoos*; 29. **IN THE COUNTRY**, *Dogging*)

EATING DISORDER BRACELETS

A teenager wearing a coloured string bracelet may be signalling to other sufferers that they have – or at least support – an eating disorder. The butterfly is a particularly popular secret charm among anorexics, and may be added to the bracelet.

- **RED STRING** Anorexia
- **PURPLE STRING** Bulimia
- **BLACK AND BLUE** Self-harm

Experts regard the bracelets as dangerous, promoting destructive behaviour as a positive thing. Be careful not to jump to conclusions, however: innocent 'friendship bracelets' also come in many colours and combinations.

WWJD

WWJD bracelets are favoured by evangelical Christians who make decisions they encounter in life by asking themselves: 'What Would Jesus do?'

KABBALAH BRACELETS

You may have seen Madonna, Mick Jagger and other celebrities wearing a red string bracelet on their left wrist. The red string is worn by some as a sign of belief in the Kabbalah, an ancient mystical offshoot of Judaism, and as protection against 'The Evil Eye'. Scholars disagree as to whether this is a true Kabbalah custom.

ACROSTIC JEWELLERY

The Victorians loved puzzles and riddles. One such was acrostic jewellery. The trick was to arrange gemstones on a necklace, bracelet or ring so that the first letter of each stone spelled out a word.

DEAR	Diamond, Emerald, Amethyst, Ruby
DEAREST	Diamond, Emerald, Amethyst, Ruby, Emerald, Sapphire, Topaz
ELISA	Emerald, Lapis Lazuli, Iolite, Sapphire, Amethyst
HOPE	Hyacinth (Zircon), Opal, Pearl, Emerald
LOVE	Lapis Lazuli, Opal, Vermeil (Hessonite), Emerald
REGARD	Ruby, Emerald, Garnet, Amethyst, Ruby, Diamond

Not all acrostic rings were sentimental. The introduction of the Corn Laws in 1815 placed a tariff on imported corn. This was designed to protect land owners but led to high bread prices and riots, demanding the laws be repealed. Support spread across all classes, as shown by acrostic rings spelling out the word R-E-P-E-A-L.

REBUS JEWELLERY

Another Victorian secret sign was the rebus, a puzzle where a word is represented by pictures or symbols. You see them in newspapers today. One rebus brooch features a crescent moon cradling a bee, standing for 'moon' and 'honey'. 'Honeymoon' brooches are said to have been given by a husband to his wife on their wedding night. In the British Museum there is a jewel featuring a bee, a knot and an 'X', standing for 'Honey, be not cross!'

LYMP BADGE

An ordinary 'little yellow map pin' (LYMP) worn in the lapel was the secret sign of Mensa, by which members could recognise each other.

For many years it would arrive as part of the membership package.

It was discontinued in the 1980s, allegedly because the US Secret Service were using similar pins to identify each other secretly when protecting the President in public!

CND BADGE

Did you know that the symbol for the Campaign for Nuclear Disarmament includes the semaphore letters 'N' and 'D'? It was created in 1958 by Gerald Holtom, a professional designer and artist, and graduate of the Royal College of Arts. During WW2 Holtom was a conscientious objector – he worked on a farm in Norfolk. Holtom also wrote to the editor of *Peace News*:

I was in despair. Deep despair. I drew myself: the representative of an individual in despair, with hands palm outstretched outwards and downwards in the manner of Goya's peasant before the firing squad. I formalised the drawing into a line and put a circle round it.

For the record, Goya's peasant has his hands up. Like Jim Fitzpatrick's two-tone portrait of Che Guevara, The CND symbol is deliberately without copyright and is used (and abused) around the world.

(*See also* 19. **IN ART,** *Che Guevara*)

Above: the semaphore positions for N (top) and D (below). Right: copyright-free protesting.

SCALLOP SHELL

The scallop shell has a 2000-year history as a symbol, from St James the Apostle to the modern petrol station.

It is the symbol of St James and is often found in churches dedicated to him. The legend goes that James saved a knight who was covered in scallops. Today we call a scallop cooked in its shell a 'coquille St Jacques'.

In the Middle Ages the scallop shell was worn as a badge of passage by pilgrims travelling to the shrine of St James at Santiago de Compostella in Spain. It guaranteed them charity at churches or inns en route. Pilgrims might also use a real shell to scoop up enough oats or barley to sustain them without impoverishing the giver.

The shell came to be included in the heraldic arms of families whose ancestors had made the pilgrimage to Santiago de Compostella, such as Prince William, Winston Churchill, John Wesley (the shell is an emblem of Methodism) – and a certain Mr Graham.

Caravaggio: *The Supper At Emmaus*

In 1897 Marcus Samuel formed the Shell Transport and Trading Company. There is evidence that both the name and logo were suggested to Samuel by Mr Graham, a fellow director who imported Samuel's kerosene into India and whose family coat of arms included the pilgrim scallop shell.

(*See also* 30. **AT THE PALACE**, *Coat of Arms*; 31. **IN A COAT OF ARMS**)

RINGS

Throughout history rings have contained hidden messages and secret signs. In 2008 a secret Jacobite ring was sold at auction in Edinburgh for £12,200. It has a concealed cipher and the inscription 'CRIII 1766 Charles Rex 1766' hidden under the emerald. It was worn by messengers carrying secret notes to and from Bonnie Prince Charlie, to prove that the notes were genuine.

Cesare Borgia is said to have owned a poison ring, with two lions whose teeth were charged with poison. Borgia would turn the ring inwards and then shake the hand of the person he wished to kill.

■ **SILVER RING THING** If you see a teenager wearing a silver ring on the ring finger of their left hand, they may be advocating sexual abstinence before marriage. The 'Silver Ring Thing' movement was started in the US in 1996 by an evangelical Christian youth minister in response to rising pregnancy and STDs among teenagers. The rings are inscribed with 'Thess. 4:3-4', i.e. 1 Thessalonians 4, verses 3-4:

God wants you to be holy, so you should keep clear of all sexual sin. Then each of you will control your body and live in holiness and honour.

The idea is that the wearer should stay celibate until it is replaced with a wedding band. In 2007 a British girl whose parents are members of the 'Silver Ring Thing' lost a case in the High Court where her lawyers had argued that the ring was an expression of her faith and not therefore subject to the school's ban on jewellery.

Rings with biblical inscriptions have a long history. A ring engraved with *Consummatum est* ('It is finished') became a charm to calm storms. A ring with the names of the Three Kings (Caspar, Melchior and Balthazar) was said to protect you against epilepsy.

■ **THE ESSEX RING** Elizabeth I is said to have given this cameo ring (on display in Westminster Abbey) to one of her 'favourites' the Earl of Essex, as a secret sign. If ever he was in trouble and needed the Queen's help, he should send the ring to her immediately.

In 1601 he was in deep trouble, having been sentenced to death for treason. Essex gave the ring to Lady Scrope to pass to the Queen. She duly gave it to her sister, the Countess of Nottingham, to deliver. But her husband, an enemy of Essex, kept the ring until Essex was dead. Elizabeth said to the Countess, 'God may forgive you, I shall never!'

FAN

It is doubtful whether the language of the fan was ever actually used. Some code-lists were published in the late nineteenth century, but possibly as a joke.

Anyway, provided you take the following with a dose of smelling salts, here are some signals to try next time you're eyeing up suitors in a formal garden:

FAN	MESSAGE
Fanning fast	I'm engaged
Fanning slow	I'm married
Handle on the lips	Kiss me
In left hand	Desirous of an acquaintance
In right hand	You are too willing
In right hand in front of face	Follow me
On right ear	You have changed
Open and shut	You are cruel
Open wide	Wait for me
Resting on left cheek	No
Resting on right cheek	Yes
Shut	I have changed
Twirling on left hand	I love another

BIHN BAGS

In 2004, bags by Washington bag designer Tom Bihn (pronounced 'bin') appeared with a secret message. The washing instruction labels read the same in each language, except in the French version, where the following was added:

NOUS SOMMES DESOLES QUE NOTRE PRESIDENT SOIT UN IDIOT NOUS N'AVONS PAS VOTE POUR LUI

With the proper accents it reads: 'We are sorry that our President is an idiot. We didn't vote for him.' Bihn claimed it referred to himself as president of the company, rather than the sitting president of either the U.S. or France.

FOREVER 21

If you're a young woman shopping for cheap-chic clothes in the US, Canada, Dubai or Singapore, you may find yourself in Forever 21, a retail clothing chain started in 1984 by Don Chang and his wife Lin Sook.

The Changs are devout Christians, which is why at the bottom of their trademark yellow shopping bags you'll find, in tiny type, the words 'John 3:16':

> For God so loved the world, that He gave His only begotten Son, that whosoever believeth in Him shall not perish, but have everlasting life

(See other 'John 3:16's in 15. **IN SPORT**, *The Rainbow Man*; 41. **IN FOOD & DRINK**, *In-N-Out-Burgers*)

3. ON THE BODY

CELEBRITY TATTOOS

Celebrity ink seems to be part of the whole fame culture, representing the celebrity's desire both to keep something private and to flaunt the mystery in public, ensuring media exposure. For example, *X-Files* star David Duchovny and his wife Tea Leoni have matching wedding-band tattoos that read 'AYSF'. According to Duchovny, it 'stands for a phrase that we say to one another, but I don't actually tell anybody'. So why mention it?

WHAT	WHERE	WHO
Elvish for '**THE NINE**' members of the *Fellowship of the Ring*	Right ankle and other places	Sean Astin, Sean Bean and other *LOTR* stars, including director Peter Jackson
Kanji character for **TANAKA**	Right ankle	TV's Superman Dean Cain (real name Dean George Tanaka)
'**100% BLADE**'	Upper left arm	Sean Bean, Sheffield United supporter
Compass with '**N, S, E, WEST**'	Ankle	David Duchovny: his daughter is called West

833	Ankle	Penelope Cruz
Ladder	Left hip	Rachel Weisz, from her days in a theatre troupe that used a step-ladder as a character
Detroit area phone code	Inner lip	Missy Margera, along with husband…
Julius 'DR J' Irving	Inner lip	…*Jackass* star Bam Margera (I hope Bam and Missy know that lip tattoos don't last very long?!)

Celebrity and ink don't always mix, given the permanent nature of tattoos and the impermanent nature of celebrity relationships. Here are some new tattoos covering up old ones!

WHAT	WHERE	WHO	PREVIOUSLY
Latitude and longitude of adopted children's birthplaces	Upper left arm	**ANGELINA JOLIE** (See right)	Ex-husband **BILLY BOB THORNTON**
Sunflower	Right buttock	**HALLE BERRY**	Name of ex-husband **DAVID JUSTICE**
'Wino Forever'	Right bicep	**JOHNNY DEPP**	For ex, **WINONA RYDER**

Before

After

SECRET TATTOOS

In 2007 a Darlington girl paid £80 to have her boyfriend's name 'Roo' tattoed on her stomach in Chinese. When she showed it off in a Chinese takeaway, she discovered that the characters actually read 'supermarket'.

Kanji characters are fraught with peril to Westerners. There are stories of people being inked with **FREE OF CHARGE** (instead of 'Free'), **AT THE END OF THE DAY THIS IS AN UGLY BOY** (instead of 'Love, Honour and Obey'), and **UNRELIABLE DELIVERY SERVICE** (instead of 'Tim'!).

PRISON TATTOOS

'Prison' tattoos that are not plain black (or blue) are almost always done on the outside.

Prison tattoos are mostly categorised as specific to their culture and environment – defining gang membership, rank, crimes committed, belief systems etc. Like an Ace of Spades for the Asian Boyz gang, or '13' for the Mexican Mafia/Marijuana use.

Here are some tattoos from the UK and US to look out for:

- **ACAB** All Coppers Are Bastards (or Always Carry A Bible)

- **AB** Aryan Brotherhood, white prison gang that originated in 1967 in the California Department of Corrections at San Quentin. Using the alpha-numeric substitution code, AB is also rendered as '12'.

  Other white power symbols include double lightning bolts and Vikings.

- **BORSTAL** An ink dot on the skin between thumb and forefinger of the right hand, earned by being sent to a young offenders' institution in the UK. In the US a triangle of three dots in the same place stands for *mi vida loca*, my crazy life.

- **CLOCK WITH NO HANDS** On upper arm, stands for doing time. Also hourglass.

- **ELBOW WEB** Indicates serious time served in prison, probably for murder, and in some places for a racist murder. In 1997, James Burmeister was convicted for the murder of two black men, allegedly in order to earn a web tattoo. He died in prison in 2007.

- **PECKERWOOD** Woodpecker, with the letters 'PW' for Peckerwood or 'APW' for American Peckerwood. Originally a derogatory term used by Southern blacks to describe poor whites, it came to mean white prison inmates, especially those prepared to fight to avoid rape or theft. Over time, the term became a source of pride for white prisoners and now refers to white youths loosely affiliated to white power gangs, and specific skinhead gangs.

Sometimes also use the three-leaf shamrock, with a number 6 on each leaf to form 666.

■ **TEARDROP** Wearer claims to have killed someone in prison (though in Australian prisons, it is forcibly inked on the faces of prisoners convicted of child abuse).

■ **13½** Twelve jurors, one judge, and a half-assed lawyer.

BRANDING

The Greeks branded slaves with the letter Delta Δ, for δουλος (slave). In Roman times, disobedient slaves were branded or tattooed on the forehead with letters representing their crime:

◆ **FUG** Runaway ('FUGITIVUS')

◆ **KAL** Liar ('KALUMNIA')

◆ **FUR** Thief ('FURE')

◆ **CF** Beware the thief ('CAVE FUREM')

In the Middle Ages offenders might receive similar brands:

◆ **V** Vagabond

◆ **T** Thief

◆ **M** Murderer

◆ **F** Fray i.e. trouble-maker

In the eighteenth and nineteenth centuries, prisoners transported from Britain to the colonies could be tattooed with marks indicating their crime, e.g. 'D' for Deserter.

Hogarth's *Taste In High Life*

AMPUTATION

When it comes to extracting tongues, splitting noses and cutting off body parts, there is no codified system. But the general principle of 'the punishment fitting the crime' often applies, especially as the visible 'sign' of punishment was a warning other people could read and understand.

Informers might have their tongues split or cut out, thieves or pamphleteers their hands amputated. People who see something they shouldn't or act shamefully in public might lose their eyes. Adulterers or sex offenders might be castrated. Ears were cut off partially or 'to the bone' for diverse offences. In eighteenth-century Jamaica, slaves convicted of non-capital offences not only had their ears cut off, but the ears were nailed to trees or the gallows.

In the Book of Judges when Canaanite king Adoni-Bezek was

defeated his thumbs and big toes were cut off – a punishment he inflicted on others – rendering him useless in battle.

In 1670 Sir John Coventry's nose was slit to the bone for making a rude remark about Charles II's partiality for actresses. In the reign of Henry VIII, the punishment for shedding blood in the King's Court was to have your right hand cut off.

BEAUTY SPOT (See left)

In the eighteenth century, wealthy men and women sometimes wore black beauty spots to hide scars left by smallpox. Satirist William Hogarth used them all the time as a secret sign of syphilis or the pox.

In the twentieth century, they came to be seen as a sign of beauty, notably on the face of Marilyn Monroe, and more recently model Cindy Crawford and singer Madonna.

BINDI

In Hinduism, the 'bindi' is a coloured mark applied to the forehead. Between the eyes is the site of the sixth 'chakra', concealed wisdom. A black bindi is the sign of an unmarried woman or widow. A red bindi indicates a married woman, and was traditionally applied by the groom during the wedding with his own blood. Nowadays, bindis can be as much a fashion accessory as a traditional body adornment and come in many different colours and designs.

SHAVED EYEBROW

Often just a fashion statement, a partially shaved eyebrow can also be a gang sign, with right or left indicating different gang allegiances, and the number of cuts indicating rank.

(See also 1. **MEETING**, *Blood and Crips*)

4. IN CLOTHES

Clothing sends out many secret signs. Apparently, red clothing increases your heartbeat and breathing whereas blue is better for interviews because it suggests loyalty. People who display brand labels have a need to belong. Men are more inclined to trust other men who wear ties.

HANDKERCHIEF CODE

Eighteenth-century 'mollies' (male prostitutes) walked around with a handkerchief poking out from between their coat-tails, as a signal that they were looking for tricks.

In the twentieth century various hanky or bandana codes evolved, indicating a staggering range of sexual activity. While the code is used far less today, the basic rule seems to be that if the guy's hanky is 'flagged' in his rear left-hand pocket, he is a 'top' (spanker, licker etc.), and if it is in his right-hand pocket, he is a 'bottom' (spankee, lickee etc.).

LEFT-HAND POCKET	COLOUR	RIGHT-HAND POCKET
Sadist	Black	Masochist
Spanker	Fucshia	Spank me
Two looking for one	Gold (three-way)	One looking for two
Tie you up	Grey	Tie me up
Diner	Lime	Table
Shaver	Red with white stripe	Shave me
Cowboy	Rust	Horse
Voyeur	White velvet	Watch me

You get the idea. The same left/right rule applies to BDSM play parties. Anything worn on the left (whip, keys, handcuff etc.) indicates 'dominant'. If they are worn on the right, it indicates 'submissive'.

CLINTON'S TIE

At the height of the Monica Lewinsky affair in 1998, prosecutors claimed Bill Clinton was using his tie as a secret sign.

White House intern Lewinsky said she gave Clinton several ties during their 18-month affair. On the day she admitted the affair, Clinton wore one of them, a navy blue-and-gold tie. The President said it was a coincidence. Kenneth Starr's team said it was a secret signal to Lewinsky, recalling their intimacy and asking her to keep silent. If so, it didn't work.

DISNEY'S TIE

If you've been to Disneyland you may have seen the 'Partners' statue of Walt Disney. On his tie there is a logo made from the letters S, T and R. It's actually the 'brand' of Smoke Tree Ranch, a small community in Palm Springs. Walt bought a house there in 1948, only to sell it again in 1954 when he hocked everything to fund Disneyland. By 1957 his theme park was a hit and Walt could buy a new home at the Ranch.

(*See aslo* 35. **IN THE PAPER**, *Dilbert*)

TEE HEE

A T-shirt with the number 420 or a leaf on it indicates interest in or use of marijuana. A smiley face is a symbol of Acid House.

British progressive-rock band Firststar hid a couple having sex in their logo (at the bottom right of the second 'T'). It duly appears on a T-shirt ironed by many an oblivious mum.

In *Lost*, the character Boone wore a T-shirt with kanji characters on it standing for '84', one of the mysterious numbers that appear frequently during the show. Charlie's T-shirt has kanji characters that stand for FATE.

RED SHOELACES

In skinhead lore, red shoelaces in your Doc Martens are a secret sign claiming that you have spilled blood in the cause. In the US, apparently, red laces mean neo-Nazi and white mean white power.

TRAINERS IN TREES

You sometimes see old trainers tied together and hanging from trees or telephone wires. The main reasons given for this are either a drug dealer 'hanging up his shield' or a gang marking its territory, plus various rites-of-passage stories.

BRITISH KNIGHT

Crips street gang members favour British Knight tennis shoes, because the BK logo can also stand for 'Blood Killas' – Bloods are the main rival gang to Crips. Note also that Crips traditionally wear blue bandannas, and Bloods red ones.

(*See also* i. **MEETING**, *Bloods and Crips*)

SPY V SPY

Puma have brought out a trainer based on the Spy v Spy characters in MAD magazine. This wordless strip features two identical spies, one dressed in black, the other in white, who are constantly trying to destroy each other – a symbol of the Cold War era. Each strip includes the Morse code:

—··· —·— ·—· ·—· · — ···· ·· ·— ···

meaning BY PROHIAS, a reference to creator Antonio Prohias. If you look closely at the trainers you can see Morse code in several places.

LONSDALE

Lonsdale-branded clothing is popular among right-wing extremists because worn under a jacket, the brand-name can be shortened to NSDA, the German acronym for Hitler's National Socialist party.

5: IN WARTIME

DANIEL PEARL

In 2002, American journalist Daniel Pearl was kidnapped in Pakistan and subsequently beheaded. During his imprisonment, his kidnappers took Polaroids of him. According to Pearl's wife Mariane, they failed to notice that he was making a secret victory sign with one hand and shooting them the bird with the other.

GIVING THE FINGER

On 23 January 1968 the USS *Pueblo* was on an intelligence mission off the coast of North Korea when it was attacked by sea and air by North Korea. The 82 survivors were held prisoner for 11 months.

In June their captors showed the men two films in which, coincidentally, North Korean camera crew were 'given the finger' by westerners. The prisoners realised that their captors didn't understand the gesture. So when the North Koreans staged photographic sessions for use in propaganda, the crew discreetly gave the camera the finger at every opportunity, signalling their opposition to the propaganda. If the North Koreans asked about the sign, the plan was to refer to it as a Hawaiian Good Luck sign.

However, on 18 October *Time* magazine revealed what the sign meant, and punishment followed. The crew was released on 23 December. The event was dramatised in the TV film *Pueblo* (1973), starring Hal Holbrook, who also referred to it in a guest appearance of *The West Wing* in 1999.

(*See aslo* 13. **IN ESPIONAGE**, *Drink Can*)

MORSE ALERT

In 1965 naval aviator Jeremiah Denton was shot down and held prisoner by the North Vietnamese for eight years. In 1966 he was paraded before the press, an event described in the citation for the Naval Cross he received:

'Forced to attend a press conference for propaganda with a Japanese correspondent, Denton blinked the word T-O-R-T-U-R-E in Morse code at the television camera which was immediately understood by United States Naval Intelligence.'.

Denton was released in 1973. He retired from the Navy as a Rear Admiral and became a Republican senator. His POW experience was made into a film, *When Hell was in Session* (1979). Denton was played by Hal Holbrook – who also played the lead character in *Pueblo* (1973), see above. In a 1968 episode of *Mission: Impossible* Jim Phelps is paralysed with curare (from a poisoned dart) but communicates by blinking in Morse code.

PORTUGUESE REVOLUTION

On 25 April 1974, a banned protest song called 'Grândola Vila Morena' by José Afonso was played on Portuguese radio. It was the secret signal for rebel officers of the Armed Forces Movement (MFA) to move against the dictatorship that had ruled Portugal for 48 years.

As the regime fell, jubilant crowds placed carnations in the guns of the victorious MFA. Every year since, 25 April is a national holiday in Portugal and is celebrated with carnations.

'WHITE CHRISTMAS'

Did you know that this Irving Berlin number sung by Bing Crosby in *Holiday Inn* (1942) and *White Christmas* (1954), played a key role in the Vietnam war?

In 1975 it was the secret signal, played on Armed Services radio, telling American soldiers to evacuate Saigon.

In March 1975, the South Vietnamese forces suffered a series of defeats by the North Vietnamese, and President Gerald Ford was advised that the capital of the South, Saigon, would soon come under direct attack. From the start of April the Americans began to evacuate non-essential personnel. On 29 April, Henry Kissinger green-lit Operation Frequent Wind. This plan, to evacuate the remaining personnel by helicopter, was signalled by playing 'White Christmas' several times on the American radio station. By the afternoon of 30 April, Saigon had fallen and was renamed Ho Chi Minh City.

MYTH ALERT

The American Presidential Seal features an eagle with an olive branch in its right talon and arrows in its left. The eagle looks to its right, towards the olive branch. You've probably seen it in the television series *The West Wing* on the carpet of the Oval Office.

There is a long-held belief, mentioned in the *The West Wing* and Dan Brown's *Deception Point*, that in wartime the eagle is turned to face the left, towards the arrows, i.e. away from a symbol of peace and towards a symbol of conflict.

This is rationalisation after the fact. The eagle originally faced the arrows, but in 1945 President Truman had the seal redesigned, so that it faced the olive branch, symbolising a country at peace. It has faced right ever since. However, the White House still has some furnishings that predate the change.

SHIBBOLETHS

A shibboleth is a peculiarity of speech or culture by which you can test whether someone belongs to your country or social group. In wartime, shibboleths are used as secret signs to distinguish between friend and foe.

In WW2 American soldiers serving in the Pacific used the word 'lollapalooza' (unusual thing or person) to flush out Japanese spies posing as Americans or Filipinos on the basis that 'L' was harder for Japanese speakers to pronounce.

In Holland the Resistance used the word Scheveningen (a Dutch seaside resort) to identify Nazi spies. After the Liberation in 1945, Allied soldiers used another Dutch place name, Nijmegen, to catch German soldiers out of uniform.

The number '77' (*sjuttiosju*) was used as a password on the border between Sweden and Nazi-occupied Norway. It is hard

contains the means to prevent the flag falling into the hands of the enemy. These include a razor blade, matches, a gun and a round of ammunition. The plan is apparently to burn or rip the flag, then either shoot yourself or slash your wrists. In some versions, items are buried beneath the flagpole.

THE VICTORIA CROSS

Every VC is made from a bronze Chinese cannon, captured from Russians at the siege of Sebastopol. Whenever a new batch is ordered, metal is cut from the 'cascabel' (the large knob at the back), and fashioned by Messrs Hancock & Co in Burlington Gardens.

Similarly, the bronze reliefs on each side of Nelson's Column in Trafalgar Square illustrating his life are made from captured French cannon from Nelson's four greatest victories – St Vincent, the Nile, Copenhagen and Trafalgar.

SOME RECENT CODE NAMES

WIDOW SIX SEVEN	Prince Harry in Afghanistan
VICTOR	Saddam Hussein in captivity in Iraq
P-DAY	Date President would decide to go to war in Iraq
A-DAY	Commencement of air strikes
G-DAY	Start of the ground offensive
MOE, LARRY & CURLY	Three areas Baghdad was divided into

6: ON THE STREET

CHINESE LANTERNS

Strung above the streets of Chinatowns across the world, the paper lantern is a silent signal of births, deaths, social events, status, joy and danger. Both colour and shape are part of the message.

Red is the sign of vitality and energy. A red lantern outside a house indicates a birth or a marriage. A plump red lantern indicates good luck as the roundness suggests the shape of yuan (money). Blue is the colour of sickness or declining energy, indicating illness in the household.

White signifies death: a doorway flanked by pair of white lanterns tells you that the family is in mourning. A special white lantern is used for funerals.

BLUE LAMP

For decades Bow Street sported the only white police lamp in London (they're usually blue so that they stand out). When Queen Victoria visited the opera at nearby Covent Garden she wished not to be reminded of the 'Blue Room' at Windsor Castle where her beloved Albert died of typhoid.

Left: Chinese lantern. Right: the blue lamp outside a police station

After 40 years of mourning, Victoria banned the colour black from her own funeral. Black horses were not used, London was festooned in purple and white, and Victoria was buried in her white wedding dress.

(*See also* 1. **MEETING**, *Military Salutes*; 26. **AT A CHURCH WEDDING**, *The Dress*)

RED LIGHT

A red light in the window indicates a brothel. It supposedly originates from the nineteeth century when railwaymen would leave their red lanterns (for signalling at night) outside a brothel during a visit. Another possible origin is the scarlet cord of Rahab.

(*See also* 24. **IN THE BIBLE**)

YELLOW RIBBONS

A yellow ribbon tied round a tree is a sign of remembrance for a loved one far away – from soldiers to convicts, emigrants to hostages.

In the past young ladies wore ribbons in their hair as a sign of fidelity. As the great ocean liners were about to depart, people on the dock would throw long ribbons up to their loved ones. As the ship pulled away the ribbons would break, symbolising both connection and separation.

The yellow ribbon is said to come from the US cavalrymen's yellow bandannas. It was popularised in the song 'She Wore a Yellow Ribbon', about a girl who wears her lover's yellow ribbon in her hair as a symbol of love and remembrance. The 1949 film of the same name starred John Wayne as a US cavalryman with a yellow bandanna. The 1973 song 'Tie a Yellow Ribbon round the Old Oak Tree' extended the concept to convicts returning home.

In 1981 the wife of one of the Tehran hostages tied a yellow ribbon round her oak tree. On the hostages' release the symbolism of the

Above left: yellow ribbon, right: Charing cross – the ultimate roadside memorial

yellow ribbon took off nationally. They have been used in response to both Gulf Wars – on trees, bumper stickers and badges.

ROADSIDE MEMORIALS

The wilting flowers tied around a telegraph pole are as much a 'memento mori' as the rotting fruit in a seventeenth-century still life.

The ultimate roadside memorial commemorates Queen Eleanor, wife of Edward I. In 1290 he erected an 'Eleanor Cross' wherever her body rested during her funeral procession from Grantham to Westminster Abbey. The one outside Charing Cross station is the 'centre' of London, i.e. the point from which all distances to or from the capital are measured.

Another Eleanor Cross in Oxfordshire is commemorated in the rhyme 'Ride a Cock Horse to Banbury Cross'.

HOBO SIGNS

During the 1930s Depression homeless hoboes wandered the dusty highways and rode the freight trains in search of work. They are said to have chalked secret symbols on houses and gateposts, telling other hoboes the sort of welcome they might expect if they asked for a meal or a bed for the night.

Among famous Americans who hobo-ed in their early lives are songwriter Woody Guthrie and screen legend Robert Mitchum.

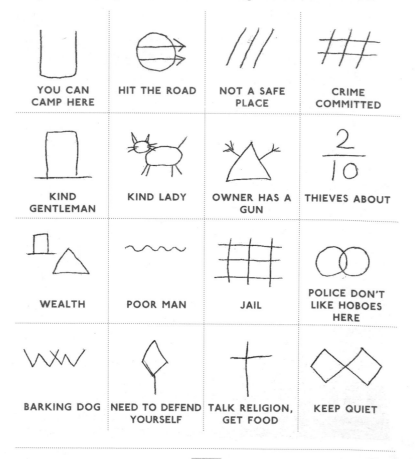

YOU CAN CAMP HERE	HIT THE ROAD	NOT A SAFE PLACE	CRIME COMMITTED
KIND GENTLEMAN	KIND LADY	OWNER HAS A GUN	THIEVES ABOUT
WEALTH	POOR MAN	JAIL	POLICE DON'T LIKE HOBOES HERE
BARKING DOG	NEED TO DEFEND YOURSELF	TALK RELIGION, GET FOOD	KEEP QUIET

GRAFFITI TAGS

A tag is the codename of the graffiti artist or 'bomber' and an expression of their art through colour and design. It tells other bombers who created the work, the risk involved and how skilled they are.

- ■ **CREW** Artists who 'bomb' together are called 'crews'. Famous crews in the 1980s include Chrome Angelz, the Subway Saints (SBS) and World Domination (WD). Today in the UK look out for pieces by 'ID', a crew of individual bombers who work together to create huge murals that satirise popular culture.

- ■ **THROW-UPS** A throw-up uses a few letters from the tag. They use less paint (mostly two colours), making them cheaper and quicker to create – useful when you're bombing a dangerous location in a hurry. Throw-ups have evolved their own art form (e.g. 'Eine' who paints capital letters in bold fonts on shop shutters) but are also used to deface ('cap' or 'dog') other bombers' work, which can cause conflict if the graffiti marks gang territory.

■ **PIECE** A 'piece' ('masterpiece') is a worked-up tag, with well-defined letters and different colours used for the outline, fill, background ('cloud') and highlighting. Using a 'shine', light appears to be reflected on the side of the letters. Other techniques add to the 3-D effect, 'popping the piece', i.e. pulling the work out of its environment. Complex works are 'burners' because they eclipse all the other works on that site.

■ **BANKSY, CARTRAIN OR CALIPER BOY?** Banksy's signature stencils have crossed the divide from meaningless defacement to collectable 'urban art'. Twenty-five years ago in New York graffiti artist Jean-Michel Basquiat, a.k.a. SAMO, did the same.

If you want to be ahead of the curve, look out for Cartrain (see right), a teenage artist from East London, who satirises politics, big business, the Royals etc. Or Caliper Boy in Shoreditch and Camberwell. His signature is a disabled Dickensian pickpocket-cum-rent boy, often with one hand down his trousers, a reminder of London's dark underbelly.

RETAIL SIGNS

According to the head of a retail chain, there are 'secret' signs that indicate the beginnings of economic decline. The first retailers to hit trouble are furniture sellers, followed by retailers in menswear, then women's wear. Next comes children's clothing and finally food.

AT THE SHOPS

When illiteracy was common, traders advertised with recognisable symbols or pictures: a sheaf of corn for a baker, a boot for a cobbler, vine leaves or holly for the pub. (*see* 7. **DOWN THE PUB**)

They weren't meant to be secret, or traders would have gone out of business! However some of the signs depended on long-lost cultural references, without which they make little sense today.

- **THREE BALLS** The pawnbroker symbol derives from the crest of the Medici family, powerful Venetian merchants in the Middle Ages who became money-lenders across Europe. According to legend, a Medici working for Charles the Great killed a giant with three bags of rocks. According to pawnbrokers, it stands for 'Two to one, you won't get your money back'.

Pawnbroking supposedly inspired the rhyme 'Pop goes the Weasel', where 'pop' means to pawn, and 'weasel' is cockney slang for coat (weasel and stoat) or suit (whistle and flute).

(*See also* 33. **OVERHEARD**, *Rhyming Slang*)

- **CIVET** The sign of a Perfume Seller was a cat-like mammal, called a civet. In the sixteenth and seventeenth centuries, perfumes were very strong as bodies were largely unwashed, and people carried pomade soaked in perfume as a protection against the Plague. The male and female civet both produce a musk prized for centuries as a fragrance and fixing agent in perfumes.

YE OLDE CIVET CAT. A·D· 1739.

Civet musk has been used in most famous brand-names and is still 'harvested', though concern for animal welfare is driving the use of synthetic alternatives. If you visit the Philippines, you might like to try Kopi Luwak, a coffee made by feeding the beans to a civet and then harvesting the partially digested remains from its faeces.

STRANGE FACT

Before he wrote *Robinson Crusoe* (1719) and *Journal of a Plague Year* (1722), Daniel Defoe made a living breeding civet cats.

■ **PESTLE & MORTAR** The traditional symbol for an apothecary was also the sign for a pharmacy. It represents the tools of the trade. Pestles and mortars were used to grind up mineral rocks and dried herbs, and for bruising roots to extract active ingredients. The symbol is still used in parts of Scotland, though the official European symbol for pharmacies is the Green Cross.

■ **RED & WHITE POLE** As well as trimming your hair or beard, barbers once offered a blood-letting service, the cure-all for pre-twentieth-century ailments.

They advertised using a red-and-white striped pole, representing the staff patients gripped during the operation, and before-and-after bandages, clean and bloody. The original poles had a brass basin at the tip, representing the bowl in which the blood was collected (or where the leeches were kept).

Barbers also performed amputations without either anaesthetic or much chance of recovery. For centuries, 'sawbones' were looked down upon by the medical profession, which is why surgeons were called 'Mr', not 'Doctor'. Today the distinction still applies, though the term 'Mr' is now a sign of respect. When Captain Kirk calls Dr McCoy 'Bones' in *Star Trek*, it is a diminutive of 'sawbones'.

AT THE NEWSAGENT'S

For pure low-tech practicality, nothing beats the 50p-a-week card display. A method of advertising that has survived intact for centuries, and remains seemingly unaffected even by the advent of the web.

It is a self-organising, simple, black market where demand meets supply. But to avoid unpleasant surprises, here are some code words to look out for...

AMATEUR FILM MAKER SEEKS EXTRAS
Best avoided unless you really want to get into the skin-flick business!

Beware any advert involving the word **SPANKING**. The 'spanking new Honda 50cc moped' may turn out to be more than you expected.

DRIVERS WANTED
Don't be surprised if your new motor is a Daimler hearse. Funeral parlours say advertising directly for hearse-drivers attracts entirely the wrong sort.

MASSAGE is fairly obvious, though ads are often dressed up with words like 'qualified NHS nurse'.

EARN EXTRA CASH! WORK FROM HOME!
Flexible hours, your own boss, up to £500 a week, sounds great. Most likely to be a pyramid scheme, where you pay £50 to sign up and only earn money getting other people to sign up. Don't touch it.

PASSENGER ESCORT
COULD MEAN HELPING OAPS ON COACH TRIPS (OR HEARSE-DRIVER!) BUT IT ALSO MEANS ACCOMPANYING ILLEGAL IMMIGRANTS HOME (e.g. TO ALGERIA).

LAYER AVAILABLE.

7. DOWN THE PUB

Pubs began as hospices for travellers run by monks. After Henry VIII dissolved the monasteries in 1536 many became roadside inns run by lay brothers. Eventually they became the social centre of every village.

Pub-signing is descended from the Roman practice of displaying vine leaves outside their taverna. In Roman Britain innkeepers used more readily available evergreens like the holly (from which come pub names like The Bush and Holly Tree). In the Middle Ages, with a large part of Britain's population illiterate, visual signs worked best – the Plough, the Star, the Bull's Head (the publican was often also the local butcher). Even today a pub sign can tell you about its history, if you know what to look for.

■ **BLACK BOY** Allegiance to King Charles II during the Commonwealth (1649–60). Charles was unusually swarthy, due to his Italian and Spanish ancestry, so 'the black boy' was his affectionate nickname. During his exile his supporters would meet and drink the health of 'the black boy across the water'. (*See Dog & Duck and Royal Oak below*)

■ **BLUE POSTS** 'Taxi rank' where you went to pick up a ride in a sedan chair. Pubs called 'The Chairmen' commemorate the poor fellows who carried the sedan chairs.

BLUE POSTS

■ **BOTTLE & JUG** Pub where you could have draught beer put in your own jug to take home – an early form of take out.

■ **CROSSED KEYS** Sign of St Peter and the Pope. After Henry VIII split with Rome, names like Crossed Keys or the Pope's

King Charles II – 'the black boy'

Head were quickly changed to safer options like the Crown or the King's Head (whichever happened to be still attached at the time!)

(*See also* 25. **IN CHURCH**, *Saintly Signs*)

- **MARQUIS OF GRANBY** a.k.a John Manners (1721–1770), son of the Duke of Rutland and Commander-in-Chief of the British Army. Loved by his men for his willingness to lead from the front, it is said that when his men were demobbed he gave them a pension out of his own pocket. Many of them used the money to open taverns named after him.

- **DOG AND DUCK** Reflected Charles II's fondness for chucking spaniels into a pond to catch mallards. Dog, Bear or Cock in the name suggest you could once find cruel sports like dog-baiting, bear-baiting or cockfighting at the inn.

- **PUNCHBOWL** Indicated the Whigs (later the Liberals) held political meetings there. Other Whig pubs include the Intrepid Fox, after Whig leader Charles James Fox.

■ **LION AND CASTLE** From the arms of Spanish region Castile y León, currently the largest autonomous region in Spain (and the EU). Probably indicated sherry-makers.

■ **RAVEN** A secret sign in the 18th century that the landlord was sympathetic to the Jacobite cause of returning a Stuart king to the thrones of England and Scotland.

■ **RED LION** Most common name in England (followed by The Crown and the Royal Oak). It originally signified allegiance to the powerful John of Gaunt, fourth son of Edward III. John's personal badge was a red lion. Later it was associated with James VI of Scotland. He ascended the English throne as James I in 1603 and ordered that the heraldic red lion of Scotland be displayed on all public buildings – including pubs.

■ **ROSE** During the Wars of the Roses (1455-1487), the painted sign for The Rose or the Rose & Crown would have indicated the landlord's political allegiance: a red rose for the House of Lancaster or a white rose for York.
(See also **28. IN THE GARDEN,** *Just Roses)*

■ **SEVEN STARS** The meaning depends on the arrangement of the stars.

A circle of six stars with the seventh in the centre indicates that Freemasons held their meetings at the inn. A circle of seven stars may be a reference to the Virgin Mary, historically identified as the woman in Revelation 12 who is 'clothed with the sun, and the moon under her feet, and upon her head a crown of twelve stars'.

Incidentally, the designer of the European Union flag, Arsène Heitz, has acknowledged that he was inspired by reference to it in the Book of Revelation.

■ **ROYAL OAK** Signifies allegiance to Charles II after the Restoration. After his Royalist army was defeated in 1651 at the Battle of Worcester, the then Prince Charles hid from the Roundhead soldiers in the 'Boscobel Oak' in Shropshire. On becoming Charles II, the King declared his birthday (29 May) 'Royal Oak Day'. It became a popular name for inns, especially those of a Royalist persuasion.

■ **THREE (CASTLES ETC.)** Pub names beginning with 'Three...' are often based on the arms of London livery companies. For example, the Three Castles relates to the masons (from the Freemasons crest), Three Compasses to carpenters, Three Kings to the Mercers etc.

■ **WHITE HART** Richard II (1367–1400) introduced legislation requiring all public buildings, including public houses, to display his emblem. At one time the White Hart was so common it was almost synonymous with 'the pub'. The most popular King's name for a pub is William IV – it was during his reign that the Beer Act came into force.

■ **SWAN WITH TWO NECKS** Traditionally swans belong to the monarch, but Elizabeth I (1533–1603) gave the Worshipful Company of Vintners the right to own a number of swans. To distinguish between hers and theirs, the Vintners' swans had two notches or 'nicks' marked on their beaks, hence the swans with two nicks (i.e. necks).

8. THE NAME OF THE ROAD

LANDSCAPE

Some roads recall lost rivers, like the Fleet, now sadly reduced to a water main beneath Fleet Street. A Cowgate was a path along which cows were led to pasture. Names with 'wall' or 'gate' in them define the older boundaries of a town or city. For example, Wall Street in New York marked the northern edge of the original Dutch town, known then as New Amsterdam. Some street names indicate their shape, e.g. Bow Street in Covent Garden, which is shaped like a longbow.

BUILDINGS

A cluster of streets with names like Abbey Road, Dean Close, The Cloisters etc. suggest that there was once a monastery on the land. Covent Garden was once a vast garden belonging to the Convent of Westminster.

EVENTS AND CELEBRITIES

'Blenheim' Streets celebrate the victory of the Duke of Marlborough in 1704. ITV's long-running soap opera *Coronation Street* celebrates the crowning of Edward VII in 1901. A 'Buller Street', such as the one in Ilkeston, commemorates General Buller, regarded in the nineteenth century as a hero of the Zulu war. 'Byron Road' is named after the popular romantic poet.

OCCUPATIONS

Wool cloth was dried on 'tenter' frames, hence street names like Tenterfield Road in Maldon, Essex (and the phrase 'on tenterhooks'). A 'Lizard' Street may indicate the land was owned by the Worshipful Company of Ironmongers (from the salamanders on their crest). Cockspur Street in Liverpool was the site of one of the city's cock-fighting pits. Lime Street or Limehouse suggests that lime kilns were once sited there. Many of the streets of Liverpool are named after both champions and abolitionists of the slave trade.

LOST STREETS

Another route into secret history is the sign of a lost street. For example, try standing on the traffic island in the middle of Charing Cross Road at its junction with Old Compton Street. Beneath the grill you can see a wall, on which there is a sign for the obsolete Little Compton Street, which once joined Old Compton Street with New Compton Street.

9. IN THE LAYOUT

KHARTOUM

The Sudanese city of Khartoum was laid out by an Englishman in the shape of a Union Flag.

It began as a military outpost in 1821, built on a spit of land said to resemble an elephant's trunk or *khurtum*. By 1834 it had become the capital of Sudan. It was sacked by the Mahdi, and then by Lord Kitchener while driving out the Mahdi. To make Khartoum easier to defend, and no doubt with a nod to Empire, Kitchener redesigned the streets in the shape of the Union Flag.

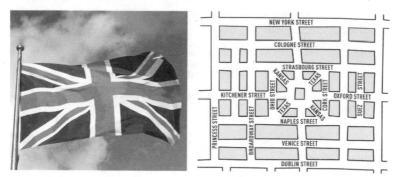

MARTINBOROUGH

Kitchener was not the only one to have this idea. The streets of Martinborough in New Zealand (above right) were also laid out in the shape of a Union Flag, by an Irish immigrant called John Martin. He named the streets after the places he had visited around the world – from Naples to Broadway to the Suez Canal. Curiously one is called Kitchener Street!

THE HOME OF SANTA CLAUS

Rovaniemi is one of several Lapland towns claiming to be Santa's home. It gets a lot of post and visitors to Santa's village, eight kilometres to the north. Though the settlement is ancient, the town was virtually destroyed by the Germans at the close of WW2. When it was rebuilt in 1947, the main streets were laid out in the shape of reindeer's antlers!

WASHINGTON DC

It is often claimed that Washington DC was designed by Freemasons, and that the street layout was deliberately designed to include Masonic symbols.

The most well-known symbols of Freemasonry are the compass and set-square, architect's tools, which for masons symbolise the Supreme Being, the Architect of the universe. The 'G' stands for geometry.

Apparently, the circle around the US Capitol building is the top of a compass. The left leg is the line from the Capitol to the White House, made up of Pennsylvania Avenue. The right leg leads from the Capitol to the Jefferson Memorial. The set-square is found by drawing a line from Union Station down Louisiana Avenue, and a similar line down Washington Avenue. Both avenues run out before the two lines join at a right angle.

Another set-square is found by drawing two lines radiating from the Washington monument, at a right-angle from each other. One line heads west to the Capitol, the other north to the White House. Continue this line north and you come to the House of the Temple, on 16th Street between R and S Streets, headquarters of the Supreme Council of Freemasonry.

George Washington, the first US President, was a Mason. So were fellow Founding Fathers James Madison and Benjamin Franklin. Within the Capitol building is the cornerstone laid by Washington wearing his ceremonial apron in a Masonic ritual in 1793.

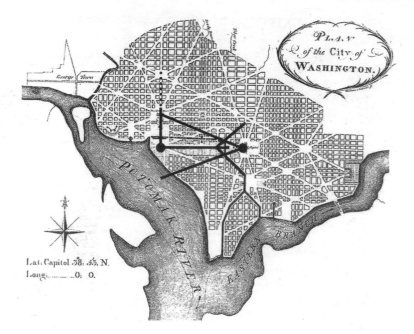

Having said that, there is no evidence that the designer of the capital, Pierre L'Enfant, was a Mason. Several of the lines said to comprise the compass and square are incomplete. Louisiana Avenue – one side of the set-square – is not on L'Enfant's plan. The House of the Temple wasn't built until 1915, the Jefferson Memorial not until 1943.

Historians believe that L'Enfant's plan – to lay a system of wide diagonal avenues over a grid of streets – was more a Baroque vision of a new republic, with neo-classical buildings reminiscent of ancient Rome.

10. IN THE SHAPE OF THE BUILDING

HAMMER & SICKLE

The Communist symbol represents the collaboration of industrial (hammer) and agricultural (sickle) workers in common cause. The Soviet Union not only displayed it on flags and buildings, but actually erected public buildings in the shape of a hammer and sickle. Surviving examples include the old GPU headquarters on Lenin Avenue in Ekaterinburg (now a hotel!) and a school in the Narva district of St Petersburg. Similar buildings were erected in Soviet satellite states as a concrete symbol of who was in charge.

> ## MYTH ALERT
>
> A discovery on Google Earth created an extraordinary urban legend in California.
>
> In 2007, the US Navy denied claims that its barracks in Coronado were intentionally shaped like a Nazi swastika. Stories were circulating that the complex had been designed by Nazi sympathisers during WW2 and the Navy never noticed.
>
> In fact the barracks were built in 1967 and the shape spotted shortly afterwards. As it was only visible from the air, the Navy decided to leave it be. Forty years on they are modifying the barracks so it no longer resembles a swastika.
>
> In 1946 the Bournemouth Evening Echo reported a truer tale. Mrs Irene Graham of Boscombe recalled how a German POW was sent every week to work in her garden. The prisoner was repatriated in 1945. The following spring, the crocuses in the middle of her lawn spelt out the words 'Heil Hitler'!

Capitol Records, Los Angeles.

TALKING JAPANESE

Another example of a conspiracy theory surrounding a building occurred in the South Korean capital Seoul in 1911. The year before Japan had defeated Korea, and the decision was made to create a new building in Seoul to house the Japanese colonial administration.

The new building was directly in front the old Korean royal palace, Gyeongbokgung, obscuring it from view. The building itself appeared to be in the shape of a kanji character: the first letter of 'Nippon', the Japanese name for their country. And the dome on top was in the form of a Japanese crown. The Japanese were expelled from Korea in 1945. Fifty years later after much public debate, the former administration building was demolished.

WHALE SONG

In Chapter 25 you'll see that churches are often built in the shape of a cross. But what about the First Presbyterian Church in Stamford, Connecticut, built in the shape of the whale that swallowed Jonah? If that seems weird to us, to a medieval worshipper it would have been deeply offensive, as the mouth of Hell was often depicted in art as that of a huge whale. (*See also* 19. **IN ART**, *Art Symbols*)

COFFIN

In Brixham in Devon there is a house shaped like a coffin. The story goes that a father was asked for the hand of his daughter in marriage. He refused, saying he'd 'see her in a coffin before she wed'. The enterprising suitor bought the coffin-shaped building, called it the Coffin House, and called the father's bluff: he would indeed see his daughter in a coffin! The impressed father gave his blessing, and the couple were duly wed.

CAPITOL RECORDS (See left)

Capitol Records in Los Angeles is shaped like a stack of LPs, whereas New York's Chrysler building is capped with a spire designed to look like a car radiator.

(*See also* 11. **ON A BUILDING**, *Morse Alert*)

II. ON A BUILDING

PINEAPPLE

A pineapple on your gate is a sign of welcome. The first European to encounter the exotic fruit was Christopher Columbus, in Guadeloupe in 1493. It remained a rare and valuable food commodity for many centuries.

In the new American colonies it became the social centrepiece of dinner parties, even though some hostesses were forced to rent them by the day! In port towns in Britain and abroad, merchant seamen might put a pineapple brought from overseas on the gatepost to show they were home and receiving guests. As a symbol of hospitality, the pineapple came to be carved onto gateposts and door lintels, incorporated into weathervanes and carpet design – even turned into follies!

This traditional meaning is lost today. The pineapple below was photographed outside a 'gated community' in Ealing.

FIRE MARKS

In the eighteenth century there was no national fire brigade to call. To insure your building against the risk of fire, you signed up with an insurance company, whose own brigade would then attend your property in the event of a fire.

To identify your property to the brigade the company would put its own symbol on your house. Some of these symbols can still be seen today. Ones to look for include the Sun, the Alliance, the Royal, the Hand in Hand and the Phoenix.

The Phoenix was created in the late eighteenth century by London's sugar bakers and refiners who found it hard to get insurance as their businesses were so prone to fire. So in 1782 they formed their own company, the New Fire Office, and adopted the Phoenix, the bird who rises from the flames, as its mark.

BRICKED UP WINDOWS

A sign that a building is older than 1851 is a window that has been bricked up or painted over. In 1696, during the reign of William III, a financial crisis brought on by conflicts abroad led to a tax on all houses with more than six windows. Many house owners responded by bricking up their windows! The crisis passed – but the tax remained until 1851.

RESCUE MARKS

In the aftermath of Hurricane Katrina rescue workers used spray paint to mark buildings they had checked. People coming home after the floods found 'X' signs on their doors along

with what was found, from a simple zero to the number of DOA
- dead on arrival.

In Montana, officials expressed sympathy – and raised money – for
New Orleans by painting thin blue lines around public buildings,
indicating the level of the flood water in New Orleans after
Hurricane Katrina struck.

THE WALL STREET BOMB

Terrorism is nothing new. In
September 1920, a bomb exploded
outside 23 Wall Street in New
York. A total of 400 people were
injured, many badly, and 33 people
died. A single warning was issued
just before the blast, signed by the
'American Anarchist Fighters', but
it is not certain who they were, and
the case was dropped in 1940.

Number 23 Wall Street was – and remains – the offices of J.P.

Morgan. As a tribute to the fallen, Morgan left the pockmarks from the blast on his building, and they can still be seen nearly 90 years later. Morgan Inc. say that the marks will stay as long as the building stands.

SHARPENING MARKS

Next time you're outside a medieval church, look for 'sharpening marks' on the walls. In the Middle Ages, men were required by law to practise archery. This was usually after the service on a Sunday, so they tended to use the stone walls to 'whet' or sharpen their arrows.

WEATHER VANES

Have you ever wondered why so many weathervanes are cockerels?

A ninth-century papal bull required the cockerel symbol to be mounted on every church and monastery in Christendom to encourage greater faith and loyalty. It was a reminder of St Peter's betrayal of Christ after His arrest. In the gospels Peter is asked by passers-by if he is a friend of Jesus. Before the cock crows twice, Peter denies it three times, as Jesus had predicted. Church-goers would have known the story and the symbolism. They also knew that churches lay East to West, so there was no need for cardinal letters (N, S, E, and W).

Other weathervane warnings against sin included mythical creatures like the wyvern, cockatrice and dragon. The dolphin is a Christian symbol of salvation, though the ones above Billingsgate Market probably relate to fish. A ship is a Christian symbol of safety in the

Probably the biggest weather vane in the world

stormy sea of life but some ship vanes celebrate specific successes at sea, from Cook's ship *Resolution* to Nelson's *Victory*.

The gilded ball atop St Paul's Cathedral is rumoured to contain Nelson's body, but he's actually below in the crypt. The Royal Exchange in the City has an 11-foot long grasshopper vane. The Exchange was built by Sir Thomas Gresham. Legend has it his life was saved by the chirping of a grasshopper. The original building was destroyed in the Fire of London (1666) but the grasshopper survived.

After the Fire Christopher Wren designed a different vane for each church he rebuilt, such as the Dragon vane on St Mary-le-Bow, whose bells define a true Cockney. Probably the world's largest vane is an actual Douglas DC3 aeroplane erected at Whitehorse airport in the Yukon, Canada.

By the way, a weathervane always points into the wind, i.e. the wind is coming from the direction in which it is pointed.

(*See also* 25. **IN CHURCH;** 26. **AT A CHURCH WEDDING**)

MOBILE PHONE MASTS

As mobile masts get smaller, it's easier to hide them in plain sight as something else. At 30 metres high they had to be added to steeples or disguised as Scots pine trees. When one such tree was planted in Beaconsfield a local resident said: 'If I want to see a plastic tree, I'll take myself off to Legoland.'

Now that masts need only be 8-metres high, they can be hidden as chimney pots, drainpipes, flagpoles – and weathervanes. The pole supporting the angel

'God, you're breaking up...'

weathervane on Guildford Cathedral is in fact a mobile mast. So is the clock on the town hall in Hungerford, and the belfry of St Stephens Church in Edinburgh.

MORSE ALERT

Many aviation warning lights on top of tall buildings flash in Morse code.

Cabot Tower Hill in Bristol was built in 1897 to commemorate the 400th anniversary of Cabot's voyage to Newfoundland. At night a navigational beacon flashes the word B-R-I-S-T-O-L in Morse code. The red beacon on top of the Capitol Records tower in LA has signalled H-O-L-L-Y-W-O-O-D in Morse since 1956 – except in 1992 when it signalled C-A-P-I-T-O-L 5-0, celebrating the company's anniversary. The original beacon was switched on by Samuel Morse's granddaughter. (See p. 66)

The beacon on Pittsburgh's Grant building flashes the city's name in Morse. The Perch Rock Lighthouse in New Brighton, Wirral, flashes a Morse roll call of local people who lost their lives at sea.

A contemporary example is Beacon Quay in Torbay. A steel ring encircles a waterfront walkway, on which lights spell out V-A-N-I-S-H-I-N-G P-O-I-N-T in Morse: a reference to the WW2 soldiers who set off into the horizon from here and 'vanished' never to return from the D-Day battles of 1944.

Finally, the light on top of the Rock of Gibraltar defiantly flashes out ——· —··· the letters GB.

12. SECRET BUILDINGS

During the Cold War this bungalow at Kelvedon Hatch near Brentwood was to be the secret centre of government and military command in the event of a nuclear attack. Beneath lies a bunker equipped for 600 people to run the country.

Power was originally supplied by generators over a kilometre away in a building disguised as a church.

How many other innocent-looking buildings hide secrets? And what are the signs that a building is not what it seems?

ONCE-OVER

A secret building may have more security cameras, and more elaborate aerials, than it seems to warrant. The door may have no handle (like No 10 Downing Street) and no letterbox (or a sealed one). If it's a suburban house, more people may go in and out than usual, while the curtains remain partially or fully closed. Net curtains may not twitch as they are often weighted at the bottom to absorb a bomb blast.

BLACKED-OUT WINDOWS

At a glance 23/24 Leinster Gardens in West London looks like a terraced house. It matches its neighbours, and has the requisite number of doors and windows.

Look closer. The windows are blacked out. The front doors have no letterboxes. The trees in front have grown unusually tall. In fact the whole edifice is just 18 inches thick, a trompe l'oeil designed to conceal the 'venting-off area' for steam trains on the District Line

23/24 Leinster Gardens from front and back

behind it. Pizza boys and posties are regularly misdirected to the address. In the 1930s people who had bought 10 guinea tickets for a charity ball turned up at the door in evening dress, only to find they had been conned.

AIR VENTS

Vents to let air in and fumes out are often disguised as something else. The Camberwell Submarine in South London is actually the ventilation system for a gas boiler complex that heats two neighbouring estates. Note the giveaway louvers.

The Camberwell Submarine

In the country, look out for strange pepperpot buildings in the middle of nowhere, which may be light or air shafts for a canal tunnel below.

During the Vietnam War, the Vietcong used tunnels to take on the American forces. To ventilate the 250-mile Cu Chi tunnel complex outside Saigon (now Ho Chi Minh City) air vents were disguised as, amongst other things, termite mounds.

ARTIFICIAL SHAPES

Another artificial mound near Bath in Wiltshire is the head of a lift leading 30 metres down to a 35-acre Cold-War city, code name 'Burlington'. It had 60 miles of road, facilities for 4,000 people to run the country, a studio for the Prime Minister to address the nation, and an underground lake to provide fresh water. Above lies RAF Rudloe Manor. In the 1990s conspiracy theorists believed Rudloe was Britain's own Area 51, where captured UFOs were kept and aliens debriefed.

CLARET TILES

One of the secret signs of a 'ghost' underground station are the claret tiles and distinctive arches on the building above.

For example, 206 Brompton Road in West London now belongs to the Ministry of Defence. Below lies

Brompton Road underground station, disused since 1934. During WW2 it was the secret HQ of London's anti-aircraft defences. Other 'ghost' stations include Down Street, which Churchill occasionally used for War Cabinet meetings, and Wood Lane, closed in 1947 and its surface building recently removed to the Transport Museum.

LEGOLAND

The least secret 'secret building' in the UK must be the fortress-like SIS (MI6) headquarters on the bank of the Thames in Vauxhall. Apart from its dramatic appearance (hence the nicknames Legoland or Babylon-on-Thames) it has appeared in several James Bond films. There are rumours of a secret tunnel under the river linking it to Whitehall.

The SIS building is almost directly opposite the M15 building, Thames House on Millbank. Thames House, previously ICI, is referenced frequently in the BBC series *Spooks*, but they actually film in the Freemasons' Hall in Great Queen Street.

Babylon-on-Thames

13. IN ESPIONAGE

CHALK MARKS

A simple chalk mark in a public place can indicate a pre-arranged message. When he needed to meet his Soviet 'control', CIA counter-intelligence officer Aldrich Ames left a horizontal chalk mark above the USPS logo on the mailbox on 37th and R Street in Washington DC.

Ames was convicted in 1994 for spying for the USSR. Among the CIA 'assets' he betrayed was high-ranking Soviet officer and double agent Dmitri Polyakov (CIA code name BOURBON, FBO code name TOPHAT). Polyakov was executed by the Soviets in 1988.

(*See also* 35. **IN THE PAPER**, *Coded Messages*)

DRAWING PINS

A group of drawing pins in a public place (a telegraph pole, door frame etc.) may indicate a 'dead drop' nearby. The positioning and colour indicates the location of the package to be collected.

In 1984 MI5 counter-espionage officer Michael Bettaney was arrested for trying to have himself recruited as a double agent by the KGB's London resident Arkady Guk. If he accepted the offer, Guk was to 'place a drawing-pin (any colour) at the top of the right hand banister of the stairs leading from platforms three and four at Piccadilly underground station.'

Guk was suspicious and never left the secret sign. The approach was reported to another KGB officer at the Embassy, Oleg Gordievsky, who was actually a double agent the other way round! Gordievsky told MI6, and Bettaney was arrested and sentenced to 23 years. Guk, meanwhile, was replaced as Head of Station by none other than MI6 agent Oleg Gordievsky.

DRINK CAN

In 1985, career naval officer John Walker was arrested for spying. He had been selling secrets to the KGB since 1967 when he walked into the Soviet Embassy in Washington and sold classified Navy communications data for several thousand dollars.

Eighteen years and over a million secrets later, Walker drove to a dead-drop site north-west of Washington DC, unaware that he was being watched by the FBI. He put an empty drink can at the foot of an electricity pole, signalling to his KGB handler that a drop had taken place. The documents were behind another pole, hidden in a bag of rubbish. The FBI picked up the can, and the documents, and Walker was arrested that night.

It is thought that the USS. *Pueblo* may have been captured by the North Koreans in 1967 (*See also* 5. **IN WARTIME**) because the KGB wanted to study equipment described in the very first documents Walker sold them.

JELL-O & THE ROSENBERGS

Julius and Ethel Rosenberg were American citizens convicted in 1951 for passing secrets about the Manhattan Project to the KGB.

Ethel's brother David Greenglass was a machinist at the atomic bomb complex at Los Alamos. Julius cut a Jell-O box in half and gave one piece to Greenglass to use as a secret sign when meeting with his KGB courier, Harry Gold, who had the other half.

The Rosenbergs were executed by electric chair in 1953.

Julius Rosenberg

CANARY TRAP

Term used by Tom Clancy in *Patriot Games* to describe a form of 'fingerprinting' where you give different versions of sensitive information to each person you suspect and see which version gets leaked, i.e. which 'canary' sang. According to Peter Wright's memoir *Spycatcher*, MI5 calls this 'Barium Meal'.

In Clancy's novel, Jack Ryan suspects a US senator or a member of his staff of leaking committee memorandums to the press. To work out who, a memo is prepared. On the summary page are six juicy paragraphs, each paragraph worded slightly differently. 96 numbered copies are made, each with a different mixture of the paragraphs. If text from the summary page appeared in the media, you could then work out which copy it came from, and whose copy that was.

Some businesses use 'canary traps' to see who is selling their mailing lists to spammers. Studios use them to protect scripts. Cartographers hide tiny deliberate mistakes in maps in order to track illegal usage of their copyrighted material, for example a non-existent bend in a road, a flourish to the end of a cul-de-sac, or misnaming an obscure lake.

In 2007, it was rumoured that Apple had planted an internal 'canary trap' about a product code named 'Asteroid' in order to identify leaks in its staff.

UNABOMBER

Not all such 'fingerprints' are deliberate. 'Unabomber' Ted Kaczynski came under suspicion when his brother David read the bomber's manifesto, published in the *New York Times* and *Washington Post* in 1995. Item 185 reads:

> *As for the negative consequences of eliminating industrial society – well, you can't eat your cake and have it too. To gain one thing you have to sacrifice another.*

Among other things, David recognised the odd phrase 'Eat your cake and have it' from an essay Ted had written in 1971. Via an attorney, David passed this information to the FBI who recognised its value. Two months later they stormed Ted's cabin. Incidentally, the term

'Unabomber' came from the FBI handle UNABOM, reflecting Ted Kaczynski's activities as a 'university and airline bomber'.

BADEN-POWELL – SPY

As well as founding the Boy Scouts movement, Baden-Powell was an accomplished spy. In 1890 he wandered around the volatile Balkans in the guise of an eccentric English lepidopterist. Armed only with a sketchbook and butterfly net, his mission was to note down the layout and fire-power of fortresses, which he then hid in sketches of butterflies and moths.

In this sketch, the 'butterfly' points north and contains the outline of a fortress. The marks on the lines show the nature and size of the armaments, i.e. fortress guns, field guns and machine guns.

(*See also* 1. **MEETING**, *Scouts;* 29. **IN THE COUNTRY**, *Trail Signs*)

Below left: the layout of the fortress. Below right: Baden-Powell's sketch indicating the outline of the fortress.

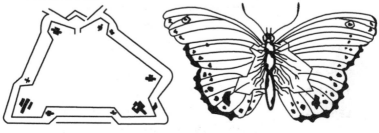

SPOOKS

MI5 stands for Military Intelligence, Department 5. Back in 1916, there were other MI departments. MI1 looked after code breaking, MI2 dealt with intelligence covering Russia and Scandinavia, MI3 the rest of Europe. MI4 was responsible for aerial reconnaissance. These and other MI departments have been absorbed into MI5, MI6 and GCHQ. MI5 is properly the SIS or Secret Intelligence Service.

■ **SPOOK TERMS** The code name for the armour-plated bullet-proof car assigned to the First Lord of the Treasury, i.e. the British Prime Minister, is 'Pegasus' (after the winged horse). Here are some more spook terms:

ASSET	Agent
BABYSITTER	Bodyguard
BLOWBACK	Unforeseen negative impact at home resulting from covert operations abroad
BOX	Secret Intelligence Service or 'MI5', short for Box 500, one of their former postal addresses (also 'The Office')
CLEANSKIN	Undercover operative with no prior record
COBBLER	Spy who creates false passports ('shoes'), visas etc.
CUT OUT	Courier who doesn't know either the agent or case officer
DANGLE	Agent who pretends to be interested in becoming a double agent, while feeding disinformation to the new agency
DRY CLEAN	To check if you're under surveillance
GOD'S ACCESS	Highest level of security clearance
THE FIRM	Special Branch
LEGOLAND	Distinctive MI6 building at Vauxhall Cross on the Thames (*See* p. 78)

LEGEND	Invented history for a cover
SHEEP DIPPING	Disguising a spy's identity with a legitimate day job
STARBURST	Losing a tail by having several similar cars suddenly drive off in different directions, making it hard to know which to follow
UNCLE	HQ of an espionage service, after the 1960s spy series
WALK THE CAT BACK	Review past events in the light of present knowledge
WET WORK	Intelligence job involving bloodshed

SECRET SERVICE CODE NAMES

The US Secret Service uses code names for prominent people and places it is required to protect and serve. For example, JFK was code named 'Lancer', Frank Sinatra was 'Napoleon', and the Department of State was and is 'Bird's Eye'.

Code names are assigned by the White House Communications Agency based at Anacostia Navy Yard and designed to be memorable and unambiguous. They are also supposed to be secret – so apologies if some of the names below have changed:

POTUS	President of the United States
FLOTUS	First Lady
VPOTUS	Vice President
TUMBLER	George W. Bush
EAGLE / ELVIS	Bill Clinton
TIMBERWOLF	George Bush senior
RAWHIDE	Ronald Reagan
TEMPO	Laura Bush
SNOWBANK	Barbara Bush

ENERGY / EAGLE	Chelsea Clinton
RAINBOW	Nancy Reagan
RENEGADE	Barack Obama
EVERGREEN	Hillary Clinton
RENAISSANCE	Michelle Obama
UNICORN / DAISY	Prince Charles
HALO	The Pope
CACTUS	Camp David
ANGEL / COWPUNCHER	Air Force One
ACROBAT / ANDY	Andrews Air Force Base
BAMBOO	Presidential Motorcade

SECRET SIGNS OF LYING

Like most of us, spies lie and are lied to. Unlike us, they lie well and for a living, and must avoid telling the truth under interrogation. So, counter-espionage agents must teach their interrogators to spot the secret signs of lying:

- **EYES** Most of us look down and to the left or right when reconstructing a memory (remembering). We look down and in the other direction when creating a memory (lying). By asking questions your interviewee is likely to answer truthfully, you can work out which direction is which, and therefore when he is lying. Liars also tend to avoid eye contact, or try very hard to maintain eye contact, especially when faced with a direct question, e.g., 'Are you having an affair?'

- **VOICE** Poor liars tend to trip over their words. You stammer, stutter or spend too long searching for a particular word. The pitch of your voice tends to rise. You clear your throat more often between answers, because it is unusually dry.

- **HANDS** Liars move their hands about more, drumming their fingers or crossing their arms. They bring their hands to their face to touch their chin, scratch their nose, bite their nails, pull on an earlobe etc. On the principle of over-compensation, liars may also keep their hands unnaturally still, shoved into pockets or trapped beneath their thighs.

■ **CHANGING SUBJECT** Liars prefer to change the subject and get onto safer ground.

(See also 14. **AT A CARD GAME,** *Poker Tells)*

14. AT A CARD GAME

POKER TELLS

A 'tell' is a unconscious secret sign by which a card-player can give away their hand.

Many tells are personal – a scratch of the nose, a tug of the ear – and you'd need to play a few times with someone to spot them. But according to expert Mike Caro, there are general 'tells' to look out for.

James Gandolfini reads 'em and weeps

A common tell is when a player acts, i.e. does the opposite of their natural reaction. If they have a strong hand, they pretend to be disappointed. If they have a weak hand, they stare at their cards as if they've got a winner. By watching a player's behaviour and then noting what they actually do next, you can quickly work out if they are the acting type.

Players who are bluffing become unnaturally still. They don't want to look suspicious so they shut down, barely breathing in case you 'call'. Players with a strong hand often look from their cards to their chips and back, because they have calculations to make. Players who fiddle with their chips probably have experience so you should be careful of them.

Of course experienced players may also use reverse-tells, pretending to give out 'tells' you then spot and act on. But as reverse-tells involve doing the opposite of the opposite of your natural reaction, it takes a lot of practice!

STARTING HANDS IN POKER

Many starting hands in Poker have nicknames. Here are some of more famous (A = Ace, K = King, Q = Queen, J = Jack):

AA	American Airlines, rockets, bullets
AK	Big Slick (from an oil spill off Santa Barbara), Anna Kournikova (looks good but never wins)
A2	Hunting season (bullet with a duck)
KK	Cowboys
KJ	Bachelor hand
K9	Sawmill hand (play it too often and you'll end up working in a sawmill)
QQ	Siegfried & Roy (pair of queens), Canadian Aces (a dig at Canada)
Q7	Computer hand (computer analysis shows it is the 'average' hand, so anything above a Q7 is worth playing)
Q3	Gay Waiter (Queen with a tray! [trey])
JK	Harry Potter
JQ	Oedipus (loved his mum…)
JJ	Hooks
J5	Motown (Jack 'n five = Jackson Five)
J4	The flat tyre (it's what you need a jack four!)
10 5	Woolworth's ('Five and dime' store in the US)
9 5	Dolly Parton ('Nine to Five' movie)
8 8	Snowmen
7 2	The Whip (if the two cards are of different suits (i.e. 'offsuit'), it's the worst possible starting hand)
5 5	Speed limit (55mph is the basic US speed limit)

Several hands are named after people if they win a World Series of Poker with that hand. For example, 10 2 is called the Doyle Brunson.

BRIDGE

In 1965 the World Bridge Championship in Buenos Aires was rocked by scandal when British pair Terence Reese and Boris Shapiro were accused of cheating by signalling secretly with their fingers.

In a match between GB and the US, Reese and Shapiro appeared to be holding their cards oddly, two fingers spread into a V. It also seemed that the number of fingers changed from deal to deal.

An investigation by the WBF found a correlation in each deal between the number of hearts held and the number of fingers holding the cards:

1 finger = 1 ♥

2 fingers together = 2 ♥ or spread = 5 ♥

3 fingers together = 3 ♥ or spread = 6 ♥

4 fingers together = 4 ♥ or spread = 7 ♥

Reese and Shapiro were found unanimously guilty. They were withdrawn from the team and their matches up to that point were conceded. However, an independent tribunal set up by the British Bridge League felt that the case was not proven beyond all reasonable doubt, especially as neither had played particularly well, and concluded that the pair was therefore not guilty.

The WBF was asked to review its judgement, and in 1967 supported its previous decision of guilty, again unanimously. Reese and Shapiro withdrew from competitive bridge, though Shapiro did return to it in his old age with considerable success. Reese wrote many authoritative books on bridge.

15. IN SPORT

TIC-TAC

The secret sign-language used by bookmakers at the race track to communicate to each other any movement in the odds and prices of a race horse. In 2008, John McCririck appeared on *Big Brother: Celebrity Hijack* and set each housemate the task of learning a Tic-Tac sign and teaching it to each other.

Right fist above left fist	**50-1**
Arms crossed, hands flat against chest	**33-1**
Fists together, right thumb upwards (like a 10)	**10-1**
Right hand on top of shoulder	**5-1**
Both hands on top of each shoulder (left on left etc.)	**9-2**
Hands in front, wave right hand above left	**4-1**
Both hands on face	**5-2**
Both hands on top of the head	**9-4**
Right hand on shoulder	**7-4**
Right hand to left ear	**6-4**
Right hand on left wrist	**5-4**

As well as hand-signals, bookies use their own private language and terminology to describe odds, horses and other aspects of racing.

AJAX	Betting tax (sometimes 'beeswax')
BIG 'UN	£1000
BISMARCK	Favourite you expect to sink without trace
BOTTLE	2-1
BURLINGTON BERTIE	100-30
CARPET	3-1 (slang for three-month prison stretch)
CHALK	Favourite (also Jolly)
COCKLE	10-1 (also Net)
DOG	Opposite of a Chalk
DOUBLE CARPET	33-1
DOUBLE NET	20-1
DOUBLE TOPS	15-8
ENIN	9-1 (reverse slang)
EYES, XS	Six (reverse slang)
FACE	5-2
HANDFUL	5-1
HEINZ	57 bets
KITE	Cheque
KNOCK	Failing to pay up what you owe
LAYER	Bookie
LEVELS	Evens
MONKEY	£500
NEVES	7-1 (reverse slang)
PONY	£25
RAG	Outsider in the field
ROCK CAKE	Small bet
ROOF	4-1 (reverse slang pronounced 'rofe')
SCORE	£20

SCOTCH	1-1 (evens)
SPREAD A PLATE	Lose a (horse) shoe
TON	£100
TIPS	11-10
EAR 'OLE	6-4

■ **OTHER SIGNALS** You can tell if the rider on a race card is a non-professional (amateur rider) because their title (Mr, Mrs, Ms, Captain, Revd etc) is put in front of their name.

HORSE NAMING

There are strict guidelines for the naming of horses, both in the UK and the US. However, a few have slipped through over the years.

There have, apparently, been a number of thoroughbreds called 'Hoof Hearted' (think about it) while 'Passing Wind' is a hurdler trained in Wales, and 'Ice Melted' is from Ireland.

'Peony's Envy' sneaked past the US Jockey Club, while in Britain trainer Thomas Tate named a cheeky little horse 'Haditovski', *Private Eye*'s nickname for Monica Lewinsky. As a joke, footballer Robbie Fowler tried to get one of his thoroughbreds named 'Another Horse' ('…and here comes Another Horse, it's Another Horse…!')

CRICKET UMPIRES

You may be familiar with the umpire's signals for 'out', 'wide', 'four' and 'six', but what about the following?

Square mime of a TV screen	**TV REPLAY**
One arm raised at shoulder height	**NO BALL**
Wrists crossed below the knee	**DEAD BALL**
Touch shoulder with hand of same arm	**ONE SHORT**
Raise arm holding ball	**NEW BALL**

Arm across the chest touching opposite shoulder	**PENALTY RUN**
Arm out, tap watch	**LAST HOUR**

LINE-OUT CODES

Before the 2003 Rugby World Cup final against Australia, the England team had their hotel swept for bugging devices. This followed suspicion that during the 2001 British and Irish Lions tour, the Aussies appeared to have cracked the Lions' line-out codes.

When a team kicks the ball into touch, both teams form parallel lines of jumpers and a player from the other team throws the ball in. The thrower uses a pre-arranged code to tell his jumpers where the ball is going, giving them the best chance of catching it. For example, each jumper is assigned a codeword. The thrower shouts out e.g. 'Postman', code for the player in the middle of the line. Other codes are more complex. For example, the team agree three words with no repeat letters, e.g. MY NEW CAR:

- **MY** signals 'front' of the line
- **NEW** signals 'middle'
- **CAR** signals 'back'

The thrower calls out a letter from one of the three words, e.g. 'Y'. This is only found in 'MY', so the ball will go to the front of the line-out.

HUT HUT HUT!

The signal a quarterback in American football gives to the other players to 'hike the ball' or start play, from a famous 1890s Notre Dame player, Jeff Hudson (Hud/Hut). It is usually preceded by numbers ('54...17...9...Hut Hut Hut!'), a pre-arranged code signalling which formation players receiving the ball should adopt next.

CORNER FLAGS AND GOLD STARS

In the English football league, only clubs that have won the FA cup are allowed to have triangular corner flags, instead of square ones. A.F.C. Wimbledon and the MK Dons both regard themselves as the only historical continuation of FA Cup winners Wimbledon FC, now defunct. But to whom does the history belong? A.F.C. Wimbledon sport triangular flags at their stadium.

David Beckham proudly sports England's one and only gold star above the badge

Only countries that have won the World Cup are allowed a gold star on their national strip.

FOOTBALL CHANTS

To a non-football fan, one of the mysteries of the sport is the chants bawled out from the terraces by fans. Who makes them up? How do they know collectively what to sing when? And above all, what the hell do they mean?

CHANT	MEANS
'All Bling and Burberry, high teenage pregnancy, no father on the scene, all robbing cash machines!'	**SITTINGBOURNE** to rivals **CHATHAM** (to tune of *La Donna e Mobile*)
'If you make a lot of money selling biscuits, buy our club.'	**WEST HAM** to their biscuit baron **EGGERT MAGNUSSON**, to tune of old 'Club Biscuit' ad
'He shoots, he scores, he'll eat your Labradors.'	To **MANCHESTER UNITED'S** South Korean mid-fielder **PARK JI-SUNG**
'Joe Royle, whatever you may do, You're going down to division two, You won't win a cup, You won't win a shield, Your next derby is Macclesfield.'	**STOCKPORT COUNTY** to **MANCHESTER CITY**, to the tune of *'Lord of the Dance'*
'He's big, he's red his feet stick out the bed Peter Crouch.'	**PETER CROUCH** Crouch is 6'7"
'When the ball hits your head and you sit in row Z, that's Zamora.'	**FULHAM** striker **BOBBY ZAMORA**, to the tune of *'That's Amore'*
'He's blond, he's quick, his name's a porno flick, Emmanuel.'	To **EMMANUEL 'MANU' PETIT**, French footballer when he played for **ARSENAL**
'The wheels on your house go round and round.'	Sung to players perceived as 'pikey'

FOOTBALL CELEBRATIONS

And if chants aren't confusing enough, what about goal celebrations? What are all those shirts-over-the-head, cartwheels and mimes of recent tabloid stories all about. Here's a rough guide:

ACTION	PEOPLE
MIMING HANDCUFFS	Tim Cahill in support of his brother Sean serving six years for GBH
SIGNS 'I LOVE YOU'	Kevin Nolan (about Bolton Wanderers)
ROBOTIC WALK	Peter Crouch has said that this is finished now
WEARING A ZORRO MASK	Facundo Sava while at Fulham
TEAM PHOTO	Chelsea's Dennis Wise
SUCKING THUMB	Luis Garcia, for first-born son Joel
ICE-SKATING IMPRESSION	South Korea's Jung Hwan Ahn, during World Cup 2002 in support of speed skater Kim Dong-Sung, disqualified at the Winter Olympics 2002

Below left: Tim Cahill. Right: Peter Crouch busts some moves.

DANCES AND LOOKS UP TO THE SKY	Ronaldinho to his dad João who had a heart attack, fell in the pool and drowned when Ronaldinho was eight
'SSHH' FINGER TO THE MOUTH OR HAND TO EAR	To fans of rival team, who have gone quiet because your team scored
ROCKING ARMS SIDE TO SIDE	New parent
POINTING INDEX AND MIDDLE FINGER DOWN AND CROSSING WITH OTHER INDEX FINGER TO MAKE AN 'A'	Support for charity called 'A-Star'
KISSING WEDDING RING	Love for wife

■ **OTHER SPORTS CELEBRATIONS** Many athletes use the 'X' sign to indicate success, crossing their arms to form an X and raising them slightly above eye level. Best not to do this in Japan or Hawaii, where it is a signal to bus-drivers that you're not taking their bus.

PEOPLE	ACTION
STEVE OVETT (Olympic runner)	I-L-Y (I Love You) with his finger after running the 800m, to his wife Rachel (they split up in 2006) (see above)
DAVE 'TIGER' WILLIAMS (NHL)	Riding his ice-hockey stick like a witch's broomstick

THE RAINBOW MAN

For many years born-again Christian Rollen Stewart was to be seen at American sports events with his rainbow-coloured wig, holding up a sign saying 'John 3:16':

for God so loved the world, that He gave His only son, that whosoever believeth in Him shall not perish, but have everlasting life.

Stewart is currently serving three consecutive life sentences for kidnapping.

(*See also* 2. **ACCESSORIES**, *Forever;* 41. **IN FOOD & DRINK**, *In-N-Out Burgers*)

MORSE ALERT

Fenway Park is the home of baseball team the Boston Red Sox. On the scoreboard two vertical stripes spell out in Morse the initials of former Red Sox owners Thomas Austin Yawkee (T-A-Y, - ·- ----) and Jean R. Yawkee (J-R-Y, ---- ·-· ----).

The only red seat in the stadium, Section 42, Row 37, Seat 21, marks the spot where in 1946, Fenway Park's longest measurable home run landed – a distance of 153m.

PURPLE SEATS

Still on baseball, Coors Field is home to the Colorado Rockies. All the seats are green except those in the twentieth row, which are purple, marking a position exactly 1 mile above sea level.

ACROSTIC BRICK

In 2004 the San Diego Padres moved to a new baseball stadium, named for their sponsors PETCO, who sells pets and pet supplies. Animal rights group PETA (People for the Ethical Treatment of Animals) had challenged the name because they questioned

PETCO's alledged treatment of animals, but to no avail. So they came up with a cunning plan.

The Padres launched a buy-a-brick campaign to raise funds for their new stadium. The bricks carry a message of your choice and go on public display. PETA bought a brick and added this message:

> **BREAK OPEN YOUR COLD ONES!**
> **TOAST THE PADRES! ENJOY**
> **THIS CHAMPION ORGANISATION**

Nice. Except that if you read it as an acrostic, i.e. the first letter of each word in order, it actually says: BOYCOTT PETCO.

BASEBALL SIGNALS

In an average game over 1,000 secret signs flash across the field. Apparently some can be traced back to battlefield signals during the American Civil War.

Sign systems are usually unique to individual teams. Still, most contain 'indicators' (a live sign is about to be given), 'wipe-offs' (negates every sign flashed so far), 'activators' (proceed as planned) and decoys (meaningless signs to confuse the enemy).

Coaches often signal by touching a part of their body, for example a different part of the chest for different moves, or hat for 'hit and run' and sleeve for 'steal'. The code may lie in the number of touches, like five taps for 'hit and run', or it might be the coach's different positions in the coach's box.

To prevent anyone learning their code, coaches may hide the real flash amid a flurry of decoys, or change the code during a game, e.g.

by swapping the sides they tap or using a different indicator. They may have more than one person flashing, and only the team know which person to look at which point.

HOOK 'EM HORNS

George W. Bush has been seen making this sign, one of the most famous in US college sports. It indicates support for the Texas Longhorns, the sports teams of the University of Texas, and is meant to resemble the head of longhorn cattle.

Unfortunately, it is also resembles *il cornudo*, the 'horned hand' supposedly a secret sign of recognition between Satanists as it resembles the head of a goat. According to this theory, Bush is the Antichrist. To find out more, type 'Bush' and 'Satan' into Google, and waste the next two years of your life.

16. IN A NUMBER

In our so-called secular age, numbers still wield magical power over us. Many skyscrapers have no floor 13, nor airliners row 13 (*See* 17 and 24 below).

For Manchester United fans the No. 7 shirt has a mythical status, having been worn by players like Best, Beckham and Ronaldo. Beckham chose No. 23 when he joined Real Madrid (and later L.A. Galaxy) because it was basketball legend Michael Jordan's number.

But numbers are only powerful if we understand their significance, and many are only meaningful to a few.

4	Unlucky in Asian culture. In Japanese, 'shi' sounds like the word for 'death'. Often replaced by 'yon', the classical Japanese word for four. In Asian countries 4 never appears in any Nokia handset model number.
5	In France 'Je te dis un mot de cinq lettres' is an insult, as the 'word of 5 letters' is *merde*, or 'shit'.
8	Very lucky in Asian culture. Prices in Chinese supermarkets (like the chain 'Super 88') often have eights in them. The 2008 Beijing Olympics officially opened at 8 p.m. on 8.8.08.
13	Unlucky in the West. 13 is linked to the Last Supper, where the 13th guest was Judas Iscariot. Friday 13th is linked to the Crucifixion, commemorated on Good Friday and therefore a day of ill fortune.

14 Hate symbol from the '14 Words' coined by white supremacist and Klansman David Lane: 'We must secure the existence of our people and a future for white children.'

17 Unlucky in Italy. There are no Row 17s on Air Italia or 17th floors in Italian high-rises. Renault R17 was renamed R117 in Italy.

18 Neo-Nazi code for Hitler (A = 1st letter of alphabet, H = 8th). 18 is used in tattoos and by Combat 18, a British neo-Nazi group. Also considered a number of the Devil, because $6 + 6 + 6 = 18$.

22 Slang French code, warning that the police are on their way: '22, v'la les flics!' i.e. Twenty-two, here come the cops!

23 'Break the line' in telegraphy code. White supremacists use 23 to represent W, 23rd letter of the alphabet and an abbreviation of 'White'.

24 Unlucky in Asian culture. Spoken aloud it sounds like 'easy to die'. Many Chinese buildings have no 24th floor.

27 Trademark of musician 'Weird Al' Yankovic. On the cover of his *Running With Scissors* album he is wearing a 27. There are 27 photos in the gallery in his *'Weird Al' Yankovic Live!* DVD.

30 Sign-off for a story filed by a journalist. May be (a) from Roman numeral XXX at end of a telegraph message, (b) early typesetting mark, (c) shorthand for 'end' in the Phillips code; corruption of the German fertig – 'finished'. In Superman comics, if someone at the *Daily Planet* fails to sign off with 30, it shows they are impostors.

39 Japanese internet slang for 'thank you' when written as a number.

40	Biblical number meaning 'a lot' rather than 40, e.g. 40 years of the Exodus, Days of Elijah's journey, Days of the Flood, Days Moses spent on Mount Sinai, Days of mourning for Jacob, Days of Lent, Days of isolation in a Roman port (origin of the word 'quarantine').
41	George W. Bush's nickname for his dad, the 41st President.
47	Appears regularly in *Star Trek TNG*, *Voyager*, *DS9* (*See also* 18. **ON TELEVISION**)
59	On a 1970s feminist badge, based on the claim that a woman earned 59 cents to every dollar earned by an equally qualified man.
68	Restaurant serving staff code. (*See* 86 below)
73	Ham radio shorthand for 'best wishes' when signing off a 'QSO' (conversation with another ham). (*See* 30 above)
77	In Sweden in WW2, '77' (*sjuttiosju*) was a 'shibboleth' password on the border with Nazi-occupied Norway. (*See also* 5. **IN WARTIME**)
81	Hells Angels, HA = 8th + 1st letter of alphabet. (*See also* 37. **ON A MOTORBIKE**)
86	Restaurant staff code for when an item is no longer available, for example '86 Chicken Kiev' or 'the oysters have been 86ed'. 68 has come to mean the opposite, an item has been added to the menu.
87	Unlucky score for cricketers: 87 − 100 −13. (*See* 111 below).
88	● Neo-Nazi sign, meaning 'Heil Hitler' (H = 8th letter of alphabet). In 2002, the Target chain store withdrew a range of in-house clothing featuring '88' as they hadn't realised it was a sign for neo Nazis.

● Slang code: two consecutive acts of oral sex (ate twice).

● Slang for 'goodbye' in Chinese SMS and IM chat. Spoken aloud, 88 is 'baba', which sounds like 'bye bye'. Very lucky in Asian culture.

● Morse code slang for 'hugs and kisses' as it looks like lips kissing.

90 Nintendo. Nintendo is affectionately known as 'Ninty' for short.

94 Boringly large number, according to *Private Eye*.

111 In cricket (and darts) a score of 111 is called a Nelson, from the incorrect notion that Nelson had 1 eye, 1 arm and 1 leg. Some batsmen (and umpire David Shepherd, right) stand on one leg at 111 to acknowledge it. A score of 111 is unlucky because it looks like a wicket without bails. For cashiers in pre-decimal UK a Nelson was £1 1s 1d.

138 Signature number of punk band The Misfits after their song 'We are 138' which is itself a reference to George Lucas' first film *THX-1138*. 138 is the name of a Misfits tribute band (*See also* 17. **AT THE MOVIES**, *More Numbers*)

152 Signature number of American band Taking Back Sunday (*See also* 32. **IN MUSIC**, *Album Covers*).

233 'Best friends forever', from the number keys for BFF.

311 Klu Klux Klan (3 Ks, the 11th letter of alphabet).

322 Part of the emblem of The Order of the Skull and Bones, a secret society of seniors at Yale University whose past members includes George W. Bush.

381 'I Love You' (3 words, 8 letters, 1 meaning).

420 ● Four-twenty is a term for marijuana or signifies you use it. In 1971 twelve pot-smoking high school students in California used it as a cryptic reference to the time to meet and light up. 420 appears on T-shirts, badges and caps. Hemp-fests take place on 20 April. The phrase '420 friendly' appears in personal ads. All the clocks in *Pulp Fiction* (1994) are set to 4:20 (*see* 17. **AT THE MOVIES**, *More Numbers*).

● 4/20 is the date of the Columbine High School massacre in 1999.

● Also a hate symbol as 20th April (4/20) is Hitler's birthday.

459 'I Love You' from the number keys for ILY.

666 666, the 'number of the Beast' in Revelation 13:18 was probably Christian code for Emperor Nero (or Domitian), who was persecuting Christians at the time. Roulette is the 'Devil's Game' because the numbers on the wheel add up to 666. 'Apocalypse' numbers have exactly 666 digits, e.g. the 3,184th Fibonacci number.

In 2007 the town of Reeves in Louisiana was finally allowed to change its telephone prefix from 666. The Mayor of Reeves called the prefix a 'stigma' and the decision to change it 'divine intervention'.

11:11 Some people claim it is more than chance that they often catch 1111 or 11:11 on digital clocks, time or temperature signs etc. They believe the number has spiritual qualities tied into concepts of 'oneness'.

1313 Bruce Grobbelaar supposedly writes 1313 beneath his autograph, for 13 years at Liverpool FC winning 13 major trophies.

2600 2600: *The Hacker Quarterly* is a magazine named for the 2600 Hertz tone once used by hackers in the US. If you transmitted this tone you could access the 'operator' mode on a call, and get free long-distance calls.

24601 In *The Simpsons*, Sideshow Bob's criminal number is a reference to Jean Valjean's prison number in *Les Misérables* by Victor Hugo.

17. AT THE MOVIES

LOST IN TRANSLATION

- In *Anchorman: The Legend of Ron Burgundy* (2004), a large sign outside a Mexican restaurant reads 'Escupimos en su alimento', Spanish for 'We spit in your food'.
- In *Top Secret!* (1984), when Nick Rivers meets Hilary for the first time at the hotel, a waiter approaches their table. He hands them menus and says: 'Gei Kahken Ahfen Yahm', a Yiddish expression meaning 'Go shit in the ocean'.

HIDDEN WORDS

In *The Lion King* (1994) when Simba, Pumbaa and Timon are looking up at the night sky, a cloud of dust appears to form the word 'SEX'. Religious groups claim this is an example of Disney slipping subliminal messages into their movies. More probably it says 'SFX' and was put in for fun by the special effects team – or it isn't there at all!

MORSE ALERT

The radio mast at the start of RKO movies is broadcasting 'RKO RADIO PICTURES' in Morse code.

Jonathan Frakes, director of *Star Trek: First Contact* (1996), claims that the blinking lights on each Borg spell the name of a different Star Trek cast or crewmember in Morse code. In *Alien vs Predator* (2004), background Morse code (mis)spells out the movie's strapline 'WHOEVER WINS WE LOSE'.

OK, it's not Morse, but the score for *633 Squadron* (1964) by Ron Goodwin has an alternating rhythm of 6 and 3 beats (d-d-d-d-d-d dah-dah-dah).

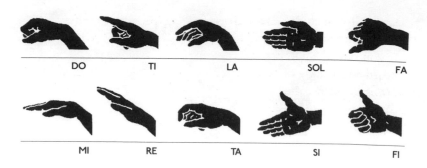

DO	TI	LA	SOL	FA

MI	RE	TA	SI	FI

TALKING TO ALIENS

In *Close Encounters of the Third Kind* (1977), scientist François Truffaut famously 'talks' to the alien with his hand. Truffaut wasn't making it up, he was using the Curwen Hand Signs (above), by which musical notes are represented by holding your hand in a different position for each note.

555

The fictitious area code used in American film and TV since the 1970s to stop people ringing real numbers (the UK uses the prefix '01632'). Nowadays 555 is used for real, but the range 555-0100 to 0199 is still reserved for films and TV.

555-2368 Who you gonna call? *Ghostbusters* (1984). Also belonged to Kojak, Jim Rockford, and the original Bionic Woman

---

555-MIKE Mike's Towing in *Transformers* (2007)

555-7643 Lisa in *Team America: World Police* (2004)

555-1013 Scully in the *X-Files* movie (1998). 1013 references Chris Carter's company Ten Thirteen Studios.

555-7583 Rachael in *Blade Runner* (1982)

555-2131 Thomas Magnum, *Magnum PI*

Some films include real numbers. In *The American President* (1995) President Shepherd gives Sydney the real White House number. If you rang the number in infomercials in *Magnolia* (1999), you heard a recording of Tom Cruise's voice in character. In *Good Will Hunting* (1997), the number on a construction company sign is that of a company in Massachusetts where Matt Damon worked during high school.

In *Bruce Almighty* (2003), God (Morgan Freeman) leaves a number which flashes on Bruce's pager – and on the big screen. Unfortunately it was a real number, belonging to a real person, and far too many people rang to speak to God.

■ MORE NUMBERS

A113 Director John Lassiter's classroom number at Cal Arts, also used by other Cal Arts alumni. See it on a cereal box in *A Bug's Life* (1998), The Master's apartment number in *Brave Little Toaster* (1987), Andy's licence plate in *Toy Story* (1995), on every plate in *Lilo and Stitch* etc.

THX 1138 George Lucas' first movie and personal signature. In *Star Wars* (1977), when Luke and Han take Chewbacca to the cells, Luke says the Wookie is a prisoner transfer from Cell 1138. In *American Graffiti* Milner's number plate is THX 138. (*See* **TANNOY** below)

CUB 1 Truly Scrumptious' number plate in *Chitty Chitty Bang Bang* (1968), after producer Cubby Broccoli. Chitty was written by Ian Fleming who also wrote James Bond, whose movies were produced by Cubby Broccoli!

37 Appears disproportionately in movies, apparently because people are trying not to choose a significant number. They choose 37 because, if you try to think of a number between 1 and 50, many people think of 37.

53 Herbie the VW Beetle's number in *Love Bug* (1968), *Herbie Rides Again* (1974) etc. 53 was the number of LA Dodgers pitcher Don Drysdale, a favourite of Love Bug producer Bill Walsh.

101 Appears on doors in *The Matrix* (1999), such as Neo's flat

CRM 114 Signature of Stanley Kubrick. 'Serum 114' was the drug injected into Alex in *A Clockwork Orange* (1971). As a tribute, Steven Spielberg put it on an amplifier in Doc Brown's house in *Back to the Future* (1985).

313 Donald Duck's number plate. In an early film *Donald's Happy Birthday* (1949), his birthday is given as 13 March (3/13). Official Disney lore makes his official birthday 9 June 1934, his debut in *The Wise Little Hen*.

420 Cannabis symbol. All the clocks in *Pulp Fiction* (1994) are set to the same time, due to the non-linear nature of the story. (*See also* 16. **IN A NUMBER**)

GRAFFITI

In *The Blues Brothers* (1980) you can see 'John ♥ Debbie' on the bridge under which the Brothers hide their car. The lovebirds are in fact Director John Landis and his wife Deborah.

There are no opening titles in *Apocalypse Now* (1979). The movie title only appears as graffiti a long way into the movie, 'Our motto: Apocalypse Now'. In *Who Framed Roger Rabbit* (1988), private dick Eddie Valliant goes into a Toontown gents, where graffiti reads: 'For a Good Time, call Allyson Wonderland'. At the end of

Alligator (1980) the graffiti in the sewer reads 'Harry Lime Lives', a reference to the character from *The Third Man* (1949) who is killed in a sewer.

(*See* 5. **IN WARTIME,** *Austrian Resistance*)

ALLAN SMITHEE

Until recently directors used the pseudonym 'Allan Smithee' to dissociate themselves from their own movie. Sometimes they disagree with the final cut, or cable/in-flight cut of their 18-certificate movie. When a longer remastered DVD of *Dune* was released David Lynch disowned it and was listed as 'Allan Smithee'. Lynch's writing credit went to 'Judas Booth' – perhaps he felt betrayed…

In 2007, Wil Wheaton (Wesley Crusher in *Star Trek TNG*) played a director called Allan Smithee in the movie *Americanizing Shelley*.

REEL MARKERS

Aka 'cigarette burns': marks in the upper-right corner of a film frame telling the projectionist to prepare to change to the second projector with the next reel. The first cue appears 8 seconds before the end of the reel. In *The Incredibles* (2004) they use the film's roundel instead.

MR AND MRS LONGFELLOW

The secret pseudonyms for two 15-foot Indian rock pythons in *Indiana Jones and the Temple of Doom* (1984). Set in India but largely shot in Sri Lanka, the film includes a scene where Kate Capshaw mistakes a python for an elephant trunk. Animal handler Michael Culling brought the pythons to Sri Lanka from Britain and booked them into a hotel under the names 'Mr and Mrs. Longfellow'.

TANNOY

Film-makers love to slip jokes into Tannoy announcements.

- The airport Tannoy in *Toy Story 2* (1999) pages 'Passenger Krich, Passenger Leon Krich' (one of the directors was Lee Unkrich); announces that 'The white zone is for immediate loading and unloading of passengers only', a line from *Airplane* (1980); and calls for 'Lasset Air, Flight A113', referring to director John Lasseter and his trademark number A113.

- In the Nazi submarine pen in *Raiders of the Lost Ark* (1981) the Tannoy apparently says: 'Eins, eins, drei, acht', German for 1138, George Lucas' signature.

CROSS-POLLINATION

In the background of *I Am Legend* (2008) a billboard shows a combined Batman/Superman emblem, release date 15 May 2010. Legend producer Akiva Goldsman has long wanted to make a movie with both DC heroes.

In *Back to the Future 2* (1989) a cinema advertises 'Jaws 19 , directed by Max Spielberg' (Steven's son). *Raiders of the Lost Ark* (1981) features R2-D2 and C-3PO as hieroglyphs in the Well of Souls. *Indiana Jones and the Temple of Doom* (1984) starts in Club Obi Wan, a reference to the mystical Obi Wan Kenobi in *Star Wars*.

WALK-ONS

In *2010* (1984), you can see Arthur C. Clarke on a park bench in front of the White House feeding the pigeons. Astronaut Jim Lovell plays the captain of the USS Iwo Jima in *Apollo 13* (1995). After the restaurant orgasm in *When Harry Met Sally* (1989), the woman who says 'I'll have what she's having' is director Rob Reiner's mum.

QUESTION MARKS

There is a superstition that putting a question mark in a movie title is bad luck which is why films like *Who Framed Roger Rabbit* and *Who Shot First* don't have them.

18. ON TELEVISION

LOST IN TRANSLATION

TV and film directors are very fond of ominous Latin chanting to create a mood. But in Japan it is often ominous English chanting! Conversely, the characters in Joss Whedon's sci-fi series *Firefly* (and subsequent movie *Serenity*) swear in Mandarin. What else has got lost in translation?

■ **SOUTH PARK** The blackboard alphabet in Mr Garrison's classroom frequently spells out rude words and phrases, for example in Spanish:

'Mi verga es fea y morena'	My penis is ugly and brown
'Chupe mis chi chis'	suck my tits
'No me toquen los huevos'	don't touch my eggs/testicles

In one episode, Cartman dresses as Hitler for Halloween. His punishment is to watch an educational film called 'Dressing as Hitler in school isn't cool'. In the film Hitler opens with the words 'Alle Menschen werden Brüder' (All men shall be brothers) from Schiller's *Ode to Joy* and an unlikely thing for Hitler to say!

■ **MY NAME IS EARL** Catalina the Spanish maid often does one thing while saying (in Spanish) another. For example, in Season 1:11 she sounds like she is swearing at Joy, but is actually saying:

I want to thank the Latino audience that tunes in to watch the show every week. And to those of you who aren't Latino, I want to congratulate you for learning another language!

In Season 6:3 after being photographed in the bathroom, Catalina says:

If you were offended by these jokes, we're very sorry but we thought they were funny.

- **STARGATE ATLANTIS** Dr Radek Zelenka regularly makes comic asides in Czech, such as 'I can't work with these actors'.

- **FUTURAMA** In the US animation about a NYC pizza boy in 3000 AD, there are two different 'alphabet codes'.

   'Alienese' is a substitution code, where each abstract character stands for a different English letter. The other is more complicated, but both are used to send secret jokes to fans willing to decode them, such as 'Venutians Go Home'. The show title is from an exhibit at the 1939 World Fair.

VULCAN SALUTE

The Vulcan salute in *Star Trek* was introduced by actor Leonard Nimoy (Spock) who is Jewish. The salute is directly related to the benedictory gesture a 'Kohen' makes with both hands during the Priestly Blessing.

LIFE ON MARS

The time-travelling cop series contains several references to *The Wizard of Oz* (1939).

DI Sam Tyler is knocked down by a car and 'wakes up' in 1973. Back in 2006 he is lying in a coma. The surgeon trying to bring Sam out of it is called 'Frank Morgan' – the name of the actor who played The Wizard in the 1939 film.

When Sam asks his boss DCI Gene Hunt if he can be transferred back to Hyde, Gene says: 'The Wizard'll sort it out. It's because of the wonderful things he does.' Gene occasionally calls Sam 'Dorothy', partly in reference to gay men i.e. the code-phrase 'Friend of Dorothy', but perhaps also as a description of Sam's predicament. When Sam has a brush with LSD, Gene says that he has 'taken a trip down the yellow brick road'. In the last episode, when Sam finally makes it back to 2006 (or does he?), the 'Oz' song 'Over the Rainbow' plays in the background.

(*See also* 1. **MEETING**, *Friend of Dorothy*; 36. **ON A CAR**, *Accessories*)

THIS IS YOUR LIFE

One of the principles of the biography show is that the subject is always surprised by the Big Red Book. To keep the whole thing a secret, each subject is given a cheesy code word, which is used until the final reveal. For example:

BEACH	Sandy Gall	Beaches are sandy
BURGER	Sir Trevor McDonald	Fast food chain
CAMP	Ruth Madoc	Hi-De-Hi
CRACKER	Frank Carson	His catchphrase
DRAKE	Clare Francis	Round-the-world yachtswoman
FIRST	Michael Winner	Winners come first
LAWN	Patrick Mower	Lawn mower
PETROL	Martin Kemp	*EastEnders'* Steve Owen ⋯⟩ S.O. ⋯⟩ Esso
POWDER	Stephanie Beecham	Beecham's Powders
ROW	Sir Jimmy Savile	Savile Row
TODD	Claire Sweeney	Sweeney Todd
YEAST	Jean Boht	Star of *Bread*

COUGHING CODE

In 2001, Major Charles Ingram appeared on the ITV quiz-show, *Who Wants to be a Millionaire*. He won the £1-million top prize, but was subsequently convicted of deception.

The court found that Ingram had cheated with the aid of an accomplice, college lecturer Tecwen Whittock. According to the prosecution, on a number of occasions when Ingram was unsure of an answer, he ran through all four options aloud. Whittock, one of the 'fastest finger first' contestants, coughed loudly when Ingram mentioned the correct option.

Whittock, Ingram and his wife were all found guilty of 'procuring a valuable security by deception'.

WALK-ONS

Since 1927 when Hitchcock first 'walked on' briefly in his own movie *The Lodger* (Hitch was actually sitting at a desk), directors and writers have occasionally appeared in their own films.

- Inspector Morse creator Colin Dexter has appeared as an extra in every TV episode of Morse and Lewis including the Bishop of Oxford in *Death is now my Neighbour*, and a college porter in *Deceived by Flight*.

- In the updated sci-fi saga, *Battlestar Galactica* leads a ragbag fleet of space vessels in search of Earth. In the fleet you can occasionally spot *Serenity*, the ship from another TV sci-fi series, Joss Whedon's *Firefly*.

- In *The X-Files* (Season 2:25) Scully is interviewed about Mulder's behaviour by an FBI agent played by X-Files creator Chris Carter. In Season 3:17, there is a brief shot of Dave Grohl, of the band Foo Fighters, walking with his wife. Dave is a friend of Chris Carter.

(*See also* **32. IN MUSIC**, *Band Names*)

CHEERS

In the final scene of the final episode, Sam the barman straightens a picture of Geronimo. This was a secret tribute to the late actor Nicholas Colasanto, who played Coach in the

first few seasons and had the picture in his dressing room. When *Cheers* ended, the cast wanted a nod to his contribution.

GERALD WILEY

Gerald Wiley, Dave Huggett, Larry Keith, Jonathan Cobbold were writers on sketch shows featuring Ronnie Barker. They were also all pseudonyms of Ronnie B.

TORCHWOOD

The secret working title of the reborn *Doctor Who*, 'Torchwood' is an anagram of 'Doctor Who'. The first two series also featured Torchwood as a running code word which cryptically referred to the alien-chasing Torchwood Institute (later to get its own spin-off series).

HEROES

A running secret sign is the mysterious helix in the US drama *Heroes*. It has appeared many times, e.g. on Jessica's shoulder (but not her alter ego's), in Peter Petrelli's stick drawing, and on the side of the pages of Claire Bear's geometry book.

47

Appears frequently in *Star Trek* franchises since *The Next*

MORSE ALERT

The theme tune of ZDF's daily news programme in Germany contains the name of the programme *Today* (Heute) in Morse.

The rhythm underlying the *Inspector Morse* theme by Barrington Pheloung taps the word M.O.R.S.E. in Morse -- --- -- .. . Pheloung says he occasionally spelt the name of the killer (or a red herring character) in the incidental music.

The late Ronnie Hazlehurst wrote the music for *Some Mothers Do 'Ave 'Em* in a hurry, spelling the show's title in Morse as the underlying rhythm.

Generation. This is a nod to a 'joke theory', devised by Mathematics professor Donald Bentley at Pomona College California in 1964, that 47 occurs in nature more often than other natural numbers. Bentley's aim was simply to introduce his students to the concept of mathematical proofs, but a Pomona alumni went on to become a Star Trek story writer, and the joke spread. Also appears in *Alias* and *Lost*.

UGLY BETTY AND ANNE BOLEYN

The necklace Betty Suarez wears in every episode of *Ugly Betty* is a copy of the famous necklace worn by Anne Boleyn.

The replica was made by Jennifer Parrish, at the request of show's stylist Patricia Field, who 'thought it would be perfect for Betty'. Many viewers of the BBC historical sitcom *The Tudors* and the movie *The Other Boleyn Girl* have spotted the similarity, though sadly some have assumed that the makers nicked the idea from *Ugly Betty*.

19. IN ART

ART SYMBOLS

Old Masters are dominated by Biblical and Classical scenes, and the symbols within them reflect this. Saints are identified by their motifs (like St Lucy with her eyes in a dish below!). Archangel Michael is clad in armour, while Cupid carries his bow and arrow. Classical figures even pop up in Biblical scenes, like the Roman poet Virgil, regarded in the Middle Ages as a Christian prophet because he 'foretold the coming of a child'.

Later medieval art widened its scope to include scenes of daily life – weddings, feasts, landscapes, mundane tasks, old age – and the symbols and allegories broadened to reflect current beliefs, proverbs and old wives' tales that people of the time would recognise and understand.

You can sometimes spot patrons painted into the picture especially in positions of piety, such as Florentine nobleman Palla Strozzi and his son Lorenzo, in *The Adoration of the Magi* by Gentile Fabriano.

St Lucy offers up
some mince pies

SYMBOL	SUGGESTS
Ape	The devil, folly
Arrow	With Cupid, love. In non-Classical painting may represent carrier of disease like the Plague
Beauty spot	Sometimes syphilis, especially in eighteenth-century satire
Blown rose	Transience of worldly wealth
Candle	Burning: God's Presence Guttering: Brevity of mortal life
Classical ruins	Brevity of life or the triumph of Christianity over paganism
Dividers	Creation of the world, Freemasonry
Enclosed garden	Virgin Mary, representing her virginity. Usually a rose garden, from which comes the 'rosary'. Mary is usually dressed in blue of innocence
Ivy	Clinging, as a wife may to her husband
Keys on belt	Power, especially worn by a woman
Lute	Lover, lust, indecency, or the transience of life
Man in a study	St Jerome
Masks	Deceit, hypocrisy
Oranges	Purity, innocence before the Fall
Owl	Folly or temptation, rather than wisdom
Ox	St Luke
Palm branch	Martyrs are often portrayed holding a palm branch, i.e. victory over painful death
Parrot	Appear sometimes in Annunciation scenes, as people in the Middle Ages thought parrots squawked 'Ave', as in 'Ave Maria'
Peacock	Juno, goddess of marriage, or Christian resurrection

Playing cards	Vice
Putti	Usually with Venus
Roses	Venus, or the Virgin Mary
Rotting fruit or meat	Still Life paintings often contain reminders that life is short – spoiling food, clocks, dying flowers, overturned cup
Skull	Memento Mori. A skull in crucifixion scenes is that of Adam, the first man, once believed to be buried at Golgotha
Sleeping	Sinfulness, sloth, especially in Dutch painting
Slipper	Vagina, love, sex
Small dog	Fidelity. In Hogarth's *Marriage à la Mode* (1745), below, the faithful little dog finds another woman's cap in the husband's pocket!
Sphinx	Lust
Stork	Children's love for their parents

Ugly people	In Classical and Mediaeval times, people believed evil caused ugliness, ergo ugly people were evil
Upset lantern	Neglect
Whale	In the late Middle Ages, the mouth of Hell was often depicted as the maw of a whale
White Lily	Purity and virginity, especially the Virgin Mary

■ SOME WALK-ONS

Albrecht Dürer	Himself, in *Martyrdom of the Ten Thousand* (1508)
Paolo Veronese	Four Venetian artists in *The Marriage at Cana* (1563): Bassano, Titian, Tintoretto and Veronese himself

DECODING HOLBEIN'S THE AMBASSADORS (1533)

This painting in the National Gallery in London depicts two ambassadors generally identified as Jean de Dinteville (left), French ambassador to England, and his friend George de Selve, Bishop of Lavaur. Embossing on De Dinteville's dagger reveals that he is 29. An inscription in de Selve's book reveals that he is 25.

At first sight it shows two wealthy and learned men in a formal setting. But there are more clues to look for:

- The objects are associated with the Liberal Arts

- On the upper shelf lie a celestial globe, quadrant, sundial and other astronomical instruments

- On the lower shelf are a terrestrial globe showing the newly discovered America (1492), a Lutheran hymnal, and a lute indicating music and love

- The floor is from Westminster Abbey, its pattern suggesting the 'macrocosm' or world as a whole, within which man, secular and religious, active and contemplative, stands as the true centre of creation

- This celebration of Renaissance Man is challenged by signs of the transience of life, like the broken string on the lute and above all, the skull

- The skull is anamorphic, a triumph of artistic skill whereby you can only see it properly by standing below and to the right of the picture. Its foreground position emphasises its message about the inevitability of death

Another interpretation places the painting within the religious upheavals of the time. In 1533, the year *The Ambassadors* was painted, Henry VIII divorced Catherine of Aragon and secretly married Anne Boleyn (already pregnant with the future Elizabeth I), leading to the split with Rome. Was the ordered world of Renaissance man about to collapse in ruins?

CHE GUEVARA

One of the world's most iconic images is that of Argentine revolutionary leader Che Guevara, created in 1968 by artist Jim Fitzpatrick from an original photograph by Alberto Korda.

But the picture contains a secret sign. Fitzpatrick recently revealed he made minute alterations to the original: he raised Che's eyes, and added his initial, an 'F' in an imaginary wrinkle on Che's tunic, lower right hand side.

Fitzpatrick has never claimed copyright on the image, as it would be contrary to Che's ideals.

He intends to hand over all rights to his image of Che to the Children's Hospital in Havana, Cuba.

(*See also* 21. **IN THE POST**, *Stamps*)

20. IN THE MONEY

BANK NOTES

The intricate designs of bank notes are very tempting to designers with a sense of mischief.

In his 250-guilder note Dutch designer Ootje Oxenaar hid his pet rabbit in the watermark. On the front of the note there is a lighthouse, at the top of which he hid the names of three women in his life: granddaughter Hannah, girlfriend Ria and a secret friend.

In his 1000-guilder note, he hid the whorls of his own fingerprint (the middle finger) in the hair of Dutch philosopher Spinoza.

Mischievous stamp designer Czeslaw Slania also designed banknotes. His Israeli note for the old 1000 shekels features a portrait of Rabbi Mose ben Maimon (1135-1204). However, his ear belongs to Slania.

(*See also* 21. **IN THE POST**, *Stamps*)

EURION CONSTELLATION

Have you ever noticed a pattern of five colour circles on a banknote? This is the EURion constellation, an anti-counterfeiting device designed by Markus Kuhn at Cambridge University.

Many colour photocopiers refuse to copy a banknote because their software detects the repeated EURions, and recognises it as a banknote.

On the 'Elgar' £20 it was disguised as musical notes, on American dollar bills as repeated number values of the note ($10 – I O, $20

– 2 O etc.). It is less hidden on Euro notes, but I bet you've never noticed!

MORSE ALERT

During WW2, from 1943 to 1945, Canada produced the 'Victory Nickel' to help promote its Allied War effort. As well as the 'V' for victory sign, there is a secret message hidden along the inner edge of the coin – in Morse code. It reads: 'We Win When We Work Willingly'

An original 1945 Victory Nickel next to the 2005 commemorative edition.

MYTH ALERT

Money is manna to the conspiracy theorists. When John Sinnock redesigned the US dime (10c) in 1946 to honour the late Franklin D. Roosevelt, people noticed the initials 'JS' below FDR's profile. In the early years of the Cold War, the rumour quickly spread that 'JS' stood for 'Uncle' Joe Stalin. The letters stood, of course, for John Sinnock.

In 1964 the same logic was applied to the new 50c coin honouring John F. Kennedy. The designer's initials, 'GS' (Gilroy Roberts), were interpreted as a hammer and sickle. The Soviets did 'plant' the Communist symbol in unlikely places (see 10. IN THE SHAPE OF THE BUILDING), but not in US currency.

If all this seems like Reds-under-the-bed lunacy, consider the theory that the $20 bill predicted 9/11. Apparently, if you fold the bill in a certain way, you will see the Pentagon and the twin towers of the World Trade Center on fire.

AMERICAN $1 BILL

There are many secret signs supposedly hidden in a $1 bill. For example, that the Pyramid and All-Seeing Eye are occult symbols of the 'Illuminati', a secret brotherhood dedicated to overthrowing governments and creating a New World Order. The number 13 is associated with the Illuminati and appears in many guises on the note, for example: 13... steps on the Pyramid, letters in 'E Pluribus Unum' and 'Annuit Coeptis', stars above the Eagle, bars on the shield, leaves and berries on the olive branch, arrows held by the Eagle.

Or that it is all about the Masons. For example, if you add a reversed triangle to the pyramid, you get a star whose points land on specific letters: A, M, N, O, S or MASON. The star can also be seen as the set-square compass symbol of freemasonry, while the 'Eye of Providence' is a Masonic symbol.

The Pyramid and Eye are certainly odd. What we know is that the two circles on the $1 bill are the two sides of the 'Great Seal' of the USA, and are usually explained like this. The 'Eye' is God watching over mankind. The 'new' nation of the USA is represented by the pyramid, as yet unfinished. The new age is shown by the rising sun, and by the words NOVUS ORDO SECLORUM, 'a new

21. IN THE POST

STAMPS

Stamps sometimes have secrets hidden in their design.

Engraver Czeslaw Slania has included himself more than once: for example, in this Swedish stamp, below left, from 1973 showing the Vasa Ski Race, he is the skier with the glasses in the bottom-left corner. Slania often included the names of his family and friends, on the spines of books or on certificates on the wall – but only visible under high magnification.

Some people believe this 1904 Serbian stamp, below right, hides a political message. The two profiles are of the King Peter, alongside his ancestor. But if you turn the stamp upside down, another face is formed, with the two nostrils as eyes and the moustaches as eyebrows. This is supposedly the face of the previous king, assassinated the year before in a military conspiracy.

During WW2, the British made French stamps with tiny alterations so that the Resistance could tell whether a letter was from an ally or a Nazi trap. Nowadays microprinting is used to combat counterfeiting, such as this 1997 Canadian stamp, below centre, where the Bear's right hind leg has an '8' hidden in its fur, and the date hidden in the grass by its right foreleg.

(*See also* **20. IN THE MONEY**, *Banknotes*)

STAMP POSITION CODE

In early twentieth-century Europe there was a fashion for using a secret lover's code on seemingly innocuous correspondence – particularly postcards – based on the position and angle of the stamp.

To write and read the code, the card was divided into 8 regions: the four corners; the middle of each side; the middle of the top and bottom. In each region, the placement of the stamps had a different meaning: upright, inverted, turned 90 degrees to the right or left and tilted 45 degrees to the right or left. Each position had a different letter/message:

A	I love you
B	Farewell my love
C	Burn my letter
D	My heart belongs to another
E	Return my love
F	I am engaged
G	Name time and place
H	Leave me alone in my grief/pain
I	Loyalty/faithfulness/fidelity is its own reward
J	You have remained/lasted/survived the trial/examination
K	Yes
L	No
M	I send you a kiss
N	I swear my eternal fidelity to you
O	Do not write again
P	Give me your friendship
Q	Do you love me?
R	Write immediately

S	Why such a long silence?
T	Meet me as usual
U	Either, be careful to act on this, or be careful to give attention to this.
V	When/how shall we meet?
W	I cannot accept your congratulations/homage
X	Your love makes me happy

ENVELOPE CODES

Most people know the meaning of S.W.A.L.K. – 'sealed with a loving kiss' – written on the back of an envelope. But how about the following wartime acronyms still in use?

BOLTOP	Better on lips than on paper (or BOLTON, N for notepaper)
BURMA	Be upstairs, ready, my angel
ENGLAND	Every naked girl loves a naked d**k
HOLLAND	Hope our love lasts and never dies
ITALY	I trust and love you
MALAYA	My ardent lips await your arrival
NORWICH	(K)nickers off, ready when I come home

Other envelope codes of less certain origins include POLO (pants off, legs open), and CHIPS (Come home I'm pregnant).

In Victorian times, the particular floral scent on an envelope or notepaper might send a message in the language of flowers (*See also* **28: IN THE GARDEN**, *The Floriography of Roses*). Nowadays, you'd be more likely to receive a text with numbers or emoticons.

☺	Smiley face
(((H)))	Big hug

@}---\-	Single rose
CSTHNKNAU	Can't stop thinking about you
CUIMD	See you in my dreams
381 OR 459	I love you

Nothing is new. A hundred years ago, 88 was slang Morse for love and kisses!

(*See also* 16. **IN A NUMBER;** 34. **ON A COMPUTER OR MOBILE**)

ELIZABETH AND DUDLEY

Robert Dudley, Earl of Leicester and favourite of Elizabeth I, is thought to have used a private symbol in his letters to the Virgin Queen. At the time of the threat from the Spanish Armada, Dudley was commanding forces at Tilbury. In a letter to Elizabeth dated 20 or 27 July 1588, he twice writes the word 'most' with two 'o's, adding a pair of small eyebrows to form a pair of eyes: mó òst. One of the Queen's nicknames for Dudley was her 'Eyes'.

LOGO AREA

In 1994 when designer Lindon Leader created the Fedex logo, he manipulated the font to include a secret arrow. According to Leader, an arrow is generally a mundane feature in advertising. What makes the Fedex arrow special is that it is a 'hidden bonus': if you don't see it you don't miss it. If you do see it, you feel good and want to tell your friends!

22. IN LITERATURE

Literature contains many examples of coded references: the little red flower with which the Scarlet Pimpernel signed his messages; the Christ figure of Aslan in C.S. Lewis's *The Lion, the Witch and the Wardrobe*; Teabing in *The Da Vinci Code*, an anagram of Baigent, co-author of *Holy Blood and Holy Grail*.

Here are a few of the many examples where writers have put secret signs, codes and symbols into their works.

HOLMES AND HOUSE

In *The Adventure of the Dancing Men* (1903), Sherlock Holmes uses frequency analysis to crack a code made of stick figures.

The figures appear in different configurations on notes sent to a woman called Elsie. 'E' is the most commonly used letter in English, and it was probable that the word 'Elsie' was used at least once in the messages. From this, Holmes is able to identify the letter E, L, S and I and work backwards from there.

Dr Gregory House, played by Hugh Laurie in *House*, was inspired by Sherlock Holmes. They both use observation and tightly argued deduction to solve conundrums. Holmes is addicted to cocaine (a 7% solution), House to Vicodin. They are both prone to melancholy, followed by near-manic activity. The number of Holmes' house in Baker Street and House's apartment is 221B. Holmes' sidekick is Dr John Watson, House's is Dr James Wilson. And finally 'House' is a pun on Holmes.

LEWIS CARROLL

The books of Lewis Carroll (real name Charles Dodgson) are full of tricks, riddles, anagrams and word-play for the initiated.

For example the Dodo in *Alice's Adventures in Wonderland* (1865) was a caricature of himself. Dodgson had a stutter and tended to introduce himself as Do-Do-Dodgson. The White Rabbit is believed to be Dean Liddell, Alice's father, notorious for turning up late for services. The Reverend Duckworth was the Duck, while the Hatter is probably Theophilus Carter, an Oxford furniture dealer known locally as the Mad Hatter because of his top hat and eccentric inventions (like an alarm-clock bed which woke you up by tipping you on to the floor!).

LOOKING-GLASS INSECTS.

In Tenniel's illustrations for *Through the Looking Glass* (1871), Disraeli is hidden as a train passenger in a paper hat. At the end of *Looking Glass*, there is an acrostic poem 'A Boat Beneath a Sunny Sky'. The first letter of each line spells:

A-L-I-C-E P-L-E-A-S-A-N-C-E L-I-D-D-E-L-L

EDGAR ALLAN POE

Poe was a keen cryptographer, and incorporated codes and ciphers in his stories, such as 'The Gold Bug' (1843). His poem of unrequited love, 'Elizabeth' (c.1829), is an acrostic, spelling her name in the first letter of each line:

Elizabeth it is in vain you say
'Love not' – thou sayest in so sweet a way:
In vain those words from thee or L. E. L.
Zantippe's talents had enforced so well:
Ah! If that language from your heart arise,
Breathe it less gently forth – and veil thine eyes.
Endymion, recollect, when Luna tried
To cure his love – was cured of all beside –
His folly – pride – and passion – for he died.

Poe drank himself to death in a Baltimore tavern aged just 40. Every 19 January since 1949, a mysterious man in black has visited Poe's grave and delivered three red roses and a half-bottle of Cognac.

(*See* 28. **IN THE GARDEN**, *Just Roses, Ann Boleyn*)

MACBETH

In 'the Scottish play' (Macbeth in theatre code) Macbeth and his wife arrange a secret signal. When Lady Macbeth rings a bell to say his night time drink is ready, it is actually his cue to murder Duncan. While he waits alone, Macbeth famously wonders:

Is this a dagger which I see before me,
The handle toward my hand?

But when the bell rings, his doubts flee:

I go, and it is done; the bell invites me. Hear it not, Duncan;
for it is a knell that summons thee to heaven or to hell.

ASTERIX

How did Asterix the Gaul get his name? According to artist Albert Uderzo it was simply because his collaborator René Goscinny wanted to make sure their work appeared first in an encyclopaedia of comics!

THE SECRET SEVEN

Though the *Secret Seven* first appeared only four years after WW2, Enid Blyton often abbreviated the gang's name to 'SS'. In *Secret Seven on the Trail* (1952), she writes that at school, all 'the Secret Seven wore their little badges with SS embroidered on the button. It was fun to see the other children looking enviously at them wishing they could have one too.'

LOGO AREA

The Amazon logo designed by Turner Duckworth is recognised across the world. But have you ever noticed the cheeky smile that forms an arrow literally from 'a' to 'z'?

23. IN A DIARY

Whether or not diaries are meant to be read, there are some things a diarist prefers to keep secret: a lover, a disability, a proclivity considered shameful at the time. Famous diarists used signs and symbols to indicate such private matters.

EDWARD LEAR

It is not surprising that poet and humorist Edward Lear kept a private diary – as the twentieth of twenty-one children, privacy must have been a rare luxury. As well as being short-sighted and homosexual, Lear suffered from epilepsy. He kept his sexuality and his epilepsy well hidden from friends but marked the epileptic attacks in his diary with an 'X'.

ROBERT HOOKE

The philosopher and inventor, friend of Wren and adversary of Newton, liked to sleep with his servants, including Nell Young, and his housekeeper Grace, who was also his niece. In his diary Hooke indicated each orgasm or sexual encounter with the Pisces symbol ♓:

- 1673 Thursday, August 21st
  Nell lay with me. ♓. Slept not well.

- 1677 Saturday, June 2nd
  Playd with Grace. ♓.

WILLIAM GLADSTONE

W.E. Gladstone was a devoutly religious man. He also had a passion
for pornography, over which he suffered great guilt. Outwardly, he
was confident and successful, becoming prime minister four times.
Privately, he whipped and scourged himself to purge his sexual
passions, and recorded each beating with a symbol of a little whip in
the diary he kept for over 70 years.

SAMUEL PEPYS

Pepys suffered no such guilty feelings, though he did write his diary
in shorthand to keep it private, and used a secret code built around
Italian, French and Spanish:

> ... and did tocar mi cosa con su mano [touch my thing
> with her hand] through my chemise but yet so as to hazer
> me hazer la grande cosa [make me make the great thing
> (orgasm)].

On 5 February 1667, Pepys managed to 'play' with a lady friend,
even though he was sitting next to his wife:

> I did come to sit avec Betty Michell, and there had her
> main, [hand] which elle did give me very frankly now,
> and did hazer [do] whatever I voudrais avec l', [would
> like with her] which did plaisir me grandement [pleasure
> me greatly].

HANS CHRISTIAN ANDERSEN

The famous Danish folk and fairy-tale writer (1805–1875) recorded
occasions of masturbation in his diary using the symbol + +.
Following a visit from such-and-such person, Andersen would
record that:

> When they left , I had a double-sensuous ++

JOHN EVELYN

A seventeenth-century gardener and diarist, was rather more
genteel, using a pentacle symbol to represent his friend Margaret
Godolphin, a young woman whom he described as 'a miracle of a
young lady in a licentious court and so deprav'd an age.' They were
both married to other people, and probably did not have an affair
– but Evelyn himself writes of his 'excessive affection' for her.

The last word, however, must go to the great French writer

VICTOR HUGO

Author of *Les Misérables*. In 1885,
at the age of 83, he marked in his
diary a symbol indicating that he
had 'possessed a woman'. The
symbol occurs eight times in thirty-
eight days.

No wonder his actual last words
were: 'How hard it is to die.'

24. IN THE BIBLE

RAHAB AND THE SCARLET CORD

The Book of Joshua (2:1-21; 6:17) tells the story of Rahab, a prostitute in the city of Jericho. In preparation for the Israelite attack, Joshua sends spies into the city to check out its military strength. When soldiers come looking for the spies, Rahab hides them under bundles of flax on her roof. In return the spies promise to spare Rahab and her family in the coming massacre, provided she hangs a scarlet cord from her window as a secret sign.

The Israelites duly sack the city, but leave the house with the scarlet cord alone. Rahab is saved, leaves her life of prostitution and marries into the Jewish tribe. Some people think the scarlet cord is the origin of the prostitute's 'red light'.

(*See also* 6: **ON THE STREET**, *Red Light*)

PASSOVER

After the Israelites have spent 430 years in Egypt, God tells Moses He is going to strike down the firstborn of every person and animal in Egypt with a Plague. To avoid this fate, the people must sacrifice a male lamb, dip a bunch of hyssop in its blood, and paint the blood on the lintel and doorposts of their houses. When the plague comes, the Lord will pass over the houses daubed with the blood.

Moses and the Israelites do as the Lord commands. The plague comes, every firstborn is killed, including the Pharaoh's son, but the people of Israel are spared. Pharaoh responds by throwing the Israelites out of Egypt – which is exactly what they wanted. This crucial event is the origin of the Jewish Passover festival.

CIRCUMCISION

The first 'covenant' God makes with mankind is when He promises Noah never to destroy the world again. The 'sign' was a rainbow. In Genesis 17 God tells Abraham He is making his second covenant. This time the sign is that 'every male among you shall be circumcised'.

Three world religions trace their ancestry to Abraham – Judaism and Christianity (through Abraham's son Isaac), and Islam (through his son Ishmael). Of the three only Christianity does not practise circumcision, and that only after a row between James 'the brother of Jesus', who argued that Christians had to be Jews first and therefore circumcised, and St Paul, who argued the opposite.

■ MERCHANT OF VENICE

Some scholars believe that in Shakespeare's *Merchant of Venice*, the 'pound of flesh' Shylock the money-lender demands of Antonio to pay off his debts is a secret reference to his foreskin, i.e. he wants Antonio to become a Jew. Another theory is that the play is a veiled reference to the persecution of Catholics under Elizabeth I.

THE LAST SUPPER

In Luke 22 Peter and John ask Jesus where they are going to eat their Passover meal. Jesus gives them coded instructions. 'Go into the city, and look for a man carrying a jar of water [a very unusual sight, as only women collected water from the well]. Follow the man,' says Jesus, 'and when he enters a house, say to the owner:

"The teacher asks you, where is the guest room, where I may eat the Passover with my disciples?" He will show you a large room upstairs, already furnished.' And it all happens as Jesus says.

It is during this Last Supper that Jesus makes the third covenant between man and God, that Judas leaves to betray Jesus, and that Jesus predicts Peter will betray him thrice.

(*See also* I. **MEETING**, *Kissing*; II. **ON A BUILDING**, *Weathervanes*; 33. **OVERHEARD**, *Shibboleths*)

DAVID AND JONATHAN

Jonathan was the son of Saul, King of Israel. In 1 Samuel 20:1-29, we read that Saul was jealous of his son's intense friendship with David (of Goliath fame). Fearing for his life, David goes into hiding while Jonathan works out whether his father is actually planning to kill his friend.

To signal which way the land lies, they hatch a plan. David will wait at a pre-arranged hiding place. Jonathan will head that way with a servant and fire three arrows nearby. If Jonathan tells his boy: 'Look, the arrows are on this side of you, collect them', then David is safe and can come home. But if he says, 'Look, the arrows are beyond you', then Saul means David harm and he must run away.

DANIEL

The book of Daniel is a secret tract. It apparently relates Daniel's fight with the Babylonian king Nebuchadnezzar (c. 630–562 BC). But it was actually written in the mid-second century BC as a coded message of encouragement to Jews suffering under the tyranny of the Persian and Greek Empires.

25. IN CHURCH

After 2,000 years at the heart of European history, Christian churches are full of signs. And in a largely illiterate culture, churches were always meant to be read 'visually'.

Churches are traditionally built in the shape of the Cross, facing East towards Jerusalem. The East window often shows images of hope, like the Resurrection. The spire draws the eye up towards heaven. Inside, many church roofs resemble an upturned boat signifying Noah's Ark, come to rest on Mount Ararat and turned upside down as a shelter.

FISH

In the early Church, the fish was a secret sign persecuted Christians used to recognise each other. In the Gospels, Jesus tells the disciples, 'Come and I will make you fishers of men', and later feeds a crowd of five thousand with five loaves and fishes. The Greek word for fish, 'ICHTHYS', formed a secret acrostic:

IESUS CHRISTOS THEOU YIOS SOTER

Jesus Christ, Son of God, Saviour

(See also 36. ON A CAR, Accessories, Stylised Fish; and Anchor below)

ANCHOR

Hope and faith in Jesus. Like the fish, the anchor symbol was also used in the catacombs as a secret sign for Christians, because the vertical and cross-bar resembled a crucifix.

For the same reasons, the Anchor was a common pub name, is often seen on gravestones, and is the badge of the Boys' Brigade. Other examples of 'crux dissimulata' or secret 'crosses' used by early Christians were the Trident, the Axe and the swastika (the ancient pre-Nazi one!).

(*See also* 7. **DOWN THE PUB**; 27. **IN A CHURCHYARD**, *Victorian Gravestone Symbols*)

VINES

You find vine leaves and grapes curling around stone pillars and woodwork. In the Old Testament the vine is a symbol of abundance. In the New, it is a symbol that Jesus uses of Himself: 'I am the vine, you are the branches'. At the Last Supper, He took the wine and told the disciples, 'This is my blood of the New Covenant' .

(*See also* 24. **IN THE BIBLE**, for previous two covenants between God and Man)

ANIMALS

Lecterns are often in the shape of an eagle, the bible resting on its wings. An eagle is the symbol of gospel writer St John and was regarded as the bird who flew the highest of all and came closest to Heaven.

The dove is not a symbol of peace, but of God's grace. In biblical times the lamb was a sacrificial animal. In churches it signifies the sacrifice of

God's Son to save mankind. Originally a pagan symbol for eternal life, the peacock was adopted by Christianity as a symbol of hope for eternal life after the Resurrection. On statues and stone knights a small dog is a symbol of fidelity. A black-and-white dog refers to a Dominican friar, from their nickname *Domini canes* (dogs of the Lord) and the colours of their robes.

You might spot a rabbit at the feet of the Virgin Mary, as a sign of her victory over lust. As well as being inveterate breeders, rabbits were considered lustful due to the similarity between the Latin for rabbit, *cuniculus* and vagina *cunnus*.

AUSPICE MARIA

In a Catholic church you may see the 'Auspice Maria' symbol, a device which combines an A and an M, and means 'Under the protection of Mary'. The symbol was also used by Mary, Queen of Scots – you can see it on her necklace in the portrait after Nicholas Hilliard in the National Portrait Gallery – and Marie Antoinette (both lost their heads!). It is also used by progressive rock band 'Dream Theater'. (*See also* 32. IN MUSIC, *Morse Alert*)

ALPHA & OMEGA

'α' and 'Ω' are the first and last letters of the Greek alphabet, symbolising that God is the beginning and end of all things (Revelation 1).

(*See also* 32. IN MUSIC, *Album Covers, Marilyn Manson / Mechanical Animals*)

SAINTLY SIGNS

You can identify saints in statues, carvings, paintings and stained-glass windows by their personal symbols.

The gospel writers are often grouped together. The symbol of St Matthew is a man or angel, Mark is a (winged) lion, Luke a bull or ox and John an eagle. The general symbol of martyrdom is the palm of victory.

(See also 27. **IN A CHURCHYARD**, Victorian Gravestone Symbols)

ANIMALS	Francis of Assisi, especially birds
ARROWS	Sebastian, after his method of martyrdom
AXE	Thomas More, by which he was beheaded
BEES	Ambrose
BREASTS ON A PLATE	Agatha, from her martyrdom. Agatha is also the patron saint of bells
CROSS OF LORRAINE	Joan of Arc (See also 5. **IN WARTIME**, Free French Forces)
HARP	David, patron saint of Wales
KEYS	Peter, to the kingdom of Heaven. Also the symbol of the **POPE** (See also 7. **DOWN THE PUB**)
LAMB	Agnes, from the Latin agnus meaning lamb
LANCE	Doubting Thomas, thrust into the risen Christ's side
MAN CARRYING THE INFANT CHRIST	Christopher, which means 'Christ-bearing' (See also 36. **ON A CAR**)
SCALLOP SHELL	James the Apostle (See also 2. **ACCESSORIES**, Scallop Shell)
WHEEL	Catherine, on which she was tortured. Hence Catherine Wheel fireworks
X-SHAPED CROSS	Andrew, on which he was crucified. Basis of the flag of Scotland of which Andrew is the patron saint

THREE

The Trinity – Father, Son and Holy Spirit – is a powerful Christian symbol, its three-part nature often depicted as an anemone, as it has three outer petals. Some anemone petals have red spots, said to represent Christ's blood, so you may see anemones in paintings at the foot of the Cross.

ALTAR

The Altar is the table on which the bread and wine of the Eucharist are prepared. It symbolises sacrifice, as an altar was where animals were sacrificed in the Temple.

In the Catholic tradition it is the focus of the building, emphasising the Incarnation of Christ, and stands in a raised position at the Eastern end of the church. For Protestants the pulpit is the focus, emphasising God's Word.

Different coloured altar cloths are used in different Christian seasons, e.g.:

VIOLET	Lent and Advent – penitence and suffering
GOLD	Easter and Christmas – celebration
RED	Martyr's days, Pentecost – blood and fire
GREEN	Rest of the year – growth

CLOTHING

Bishops wear purple, the colour of kings and emperors since Roman times. They carry a crozier or shepherd's crook to symbolise Christ as the good Shepherd.

The acorn on the cord of a Cardinal's hat symbolises fecundity, prosperity and spiritual growth. The three knots in a monk's belt represent their vows of poverty, chastity and obedience. The word 'cappuccino' comes from the brown and white habit of Capucin monks. A nun's veil symbolises protection and separation, possibly from the veils worn by temple virgins in Greek and Roman temples.

CANTUAR+

In the Church of England, bishops and archbishops sign their names using a Latinised version of their see, and a cross. At the time of writing, the Archbishop of Canterbury becomes Rowan Cantuar+. The Archbishop of York is John Ebor+, the Bishop of Rochester is Michael Roffen+.

SIGN LANGUAGE

Just because a monastic order is partially or wholly silent, it doesn't mean they don't communicate. The Benedictines have over a hundred secret signs for silent occasions, e.g.

KING	Turn your hand downwards and hold the top of it with all the fingers of the other hand to make the sign of a crown
THE DEAN	Let your hand hang down and pretend to ring a small bell
NUN	Put your two index fingers in front of your head and stroke down your cheeks to signal the veil
LAYMAN	Pull your chin as if tugging a beard (monks were clean-shaven, unlike laymen)
PASS ME A MASS VESTMENT	Stroke your outspread hands down your chest
PASS ME THE FISH	Move your hand like a fish swimming
PASS THE SALT	Stroke your hands with three fingers together
I NEED A KNIFE	Cut with one finger over another

GARGOYLES

The word 'gargoyle' comes from the French 'gargouille', meaning throat or pipe (as do the words 'gargle' and 'gurgle'). It is a spout that runs off excess water from the roofs of buildings. As they were far from the ground, mischievous masons could fashion fabulous creatures, pagan icons, familiar faces, even defecating gargoyles. In the twelfth century, St Bernard of Clairvaux asked:

> *What are these fantastic monsters doing in the cloisters under the very eyes of the brothers as they read? What is the meaning of these unclean monkeys, strange savage lions and monsters?*

To medieval minds a church was a 'sermon in stone'. Gargoyles reminded people of the reality of the supernatural. Some were characters from Bible stories. Others were frightening creatures designed to ward off evil spirits, or to remind church-goers of the continuous presence of evil in the world.

Just as Christianity incorporated earlier pagan sites and festivals to facilitate conversion, so it incorporated the creatures of mythology into its temples. Gargoyles pull open their mouths and stick out their tongues, like giants who can swallow you up. Men with foliage represent the Green Man. Even pagan fertility symbols can be found, carved on the roofs to scare away evil spirits.

Masons also carved more mundane secrets into their gargoyles, representing themselves or their friends in stone, while grotesque figures or faces might resemble a local busybody or an officious cleric.

■ **LIVING GARGOYLES** In 1996, an ecclesiastical court allowed two living clerics to be immortalised in stone, at St Peter's Oundle. Bill Westwood, former Bishop of Peterborough, and Canon Lloyd Caddick, the church's former vicar, were depicted as small limestone carvings in the thirteenth-century church. Four parishioners had argued that gargoyles should only be made of the dead.

In 2007 stonemason Gardner Molloy was restoring sixteenth-century gargoyles at Lennoxlove House in East Lothian, when he heard his father had died in an accident. As a tribute Molloy depicted the final gargoyle on the tallest tower as his 86-year-old dad. Molloy's mother Inez, who died in 2002, is commemorated in the sign on the National Gallery of Scotland in Edinburgh. While working on the sign, Molloy secretly carved her name and dates into the base of a letter 'I' – for Inez.

26. AT A CHURCH WEDDING

If you decode a Church wedding you will realise that they are all about avoiding bad luck and encouraging fertility.

LUCK

You know it is bad luck for the groom to see the dress before the wedding? Well, there's a lot more that's unlucky about weddings:

- Getting married in May, or during Lent
- Getting married on a Thursday, Friday or Saturday ('Thursday for losses, Friday for crosses, Saturday for no luck at all')
- Forgetting to return the 'something borrowed'
- Getting married in green, pink, grey, purple, black or red ('Marry in red you'll wish yourself dead')
- Making your own dress or wearing it in full before the Big Day
- Having a bouquet of red and white flowers
- Seeing an open grave, a pig, a monk or a nun on the way to church
- Dropping the ring during the ceremony (especially if it lands on a gravestone)

FERTILITY

In the past to encourage fertility:

- The couple got married in April (Spring) or June (after Juno, goddess of love and marriage)
- Guests brought gifts of fruit (a distant echo of the modern wedding list)

- The couple were showered with rice, or flower petals or sweets
- In Scotland a lactating woman prepared the honeymoon bed
- In Ireland, a laying hen was tied to it

RINGS

We probably have the Romans to thank for the engagement ring, though their simple iron band was more a symbol of ownership than love. In colonial America where jewellery was frowned upon, the practical thimble was given as a token of love.

The wedding ring symbolises eternity. In ancient Egypt the circle signified immortality and eternal love, especially as a hooped serpent with its tail in its mouth. The fourth finger was thought to contain a special vein connected directly to the heart. More recently, a diamond in a ring is another symbol of eternity.

(*See also 2.* **ACCESSORIES**, *Rings*)

SOMETHING BORROWED...

- 'Something old' – link to the past, e.g. grandmother's wedding ring
- 'Something new' – promise of the future, e.g. the new wedding dress
- 'Something borrowed' – reminder of continued support from friends and family, e.g. a handkerchief
- 'Something blue' – symbol of faithfulness and purity, e.g. bride's garter
- 'And a silver sixpence in her shoe'

(*See also 36.* **ON A CAR**, *Accessories, Blue Garter*)

THE DRESS

The white dress is relatively modern. Queen Victoria started a trend by marrying in a silk white dress, instead of the traditional Royal silver. Also the Victorians liked to show off – such an impractical colour could only be worn once. Before White, brides wore their best dresses, preferably of blue, pearl or brown.

The dress shouldn't be (quite) finished until the last moment. No wonder the bride is always late…

BRIDESMAIDS

Like the veil, the bridesmaids are there to protect the bride from malevolent spirits. Just as the veil prevents the evil ones from seeing the bride, so the maids confuse them by dressing the same.

THE CEREMONY

The bride stands to the groom's left during the ceremony to allow his sword arm to be free. Many people don't realise the exchange of rings in the sight of God is the actual 'sign' that the marriage has taken place. The priest merely confirms this when he or she declares the couple husband and wife.

BEST MAN

As well as protecting the groom (why does everyone need protection?) he must remember to pay the church's fee in an odd sum, to bring the couple good luck.

THE CAKE

Medieval wedding guests each brought a small fruit and nut cake (symbol of fruitfulness!) which were stacked up on the table. It was a sign of good luck if the bride and groom could kiss across the pile. Another claim is that the tiered design is the work of a seventeenth-century baker inspired (pun intended) by the spire of St. Brides Church in Fleet Street, rebuilt by Christopher Wren after the Fire of London in 1666.

Right: St. Brides church spire

AFTER THE CEREMONY

The groom carries the bride over the threshold through the main entrance of their new home to protect her from lurking evil spirits. Phew, they made it!

27. IN A CHURCHYARD

Old churchyards can be really fun (really!) because they are full of secret signs.

YEW TREE

The ubiquitous yew tree is said to have been a pre-Christian symbol associated with druids and with death, as they are very poisonous. Some people believe churches were built on pagan sites and 'inherited' the yews. However the yew has been a Christian symbol for centuries. Like the holly it is evergreen and bears red berries, both symbols of the Crucifixion and Resurrection. Its medieval associations with death were also practical – the poisonous bark and needles killed wandering livestock, and wood from the yew tree was the staple material for the English longbow.

LYCH-GATE

The lych-gate at the entrance dates back to the Middle Ages. It was where the clergyman met the funeral procession and the corpse was rested, usually in a shroud. Lych means 'corpse'.

BURIAL SITE

Christians are usually buried with their feet facing east and their heads west. Priests are usually buried the other way round so that on Judgement Day they face their congregation.

The south side of a church was considered more 'holy', as the north is often in shadow. As a consequence, you are more likely to find the graves of criminals, suicides and unbaptised babies on the north side of the church.

GRAVESTONES

Few gravestones survive from the seventeenth century or before (pre-Reformation markers were wooden), so the majority of older stones in a churchyard tend to be Victorian. Which is fortunate for secret-sign spotters, because the Victorians loved their symbols.

Some are familiar from other contexts, such as the circle of the Celtic cross as a sign of eternity, or the Masonic set-square and compasses. Others, like a lamb indicating the death of a child, are less familiar.

■ VICTORIAN GRAVESTONE SYMBOLS

ANCHOR (& CHAIN)	Hope (a disguised cross)
ANT	Industrious person
BEE, BEEHIVE	Resurrection, chastity
BROKEN COLUMN	Cut off in the prime of life, especially head of the family
BROKEN FLOWER	Sudden or early death
BUTTERFLY	Resurrection
CLASPED HANDS	Friendship and fidelity for ever
CROSSED SWORDS	High-ranked military person
CROZIER	Bishop (a shepherd's crook)

HAND (OF GOD) POINTING DOWN	Mortality or sudden death
HOURGLASS	Mortality, transience of life (also Grim Reaper, skull & bones, snuffed candle, Father Time etc.)
LAMB	Common Victorian marker for a child, the lamb is Christ who redeems through His sacrifice
LILY	Chastity or innocence, may indicate a baby or maiden
LION	May have been a fallen hero
OBELISK	Egyptian symbol for life and health
OPEN BIBLE	Clergyman
PALM	Symbol of martyrdom
PINEAPPLE	Hospitable person (*See also* 11: ON A BUILDING)
POPPY	Peace and Rest (from its use as opium). Note the Christian 'fish' hidden in the poppy stems
SET SQUARE & COMPASS	Mason and/or architect
SEVERED BUD	Child
THISTLE	Of Scottish descent (Tudor Rose for English)
TORCH, UPSIDE DOWN	Life literally snuffed out
WHEAT GATHERED	Harvest, often a death in the 'autumn' of life

1. Torches upside down 2. Poppies
3. Broken column 4. Lillies,
5. Hourglass 6. Wheatsheaf
7. Clasped hands and 8. Clasped
hands close up.

⌐◻⌐◻⌐◻◻◻⌐◻◻◻⌐

SECRET CODE

As well as Masonic symbols the stone of James Leeson in the graveyard of Trinity Church New York bears a series a cryptic box-and-dot symbols around the upper edge (see above). Leeson, a butcher and tavern-keeper, died in 1792 (the burial ground dates back to the Dutch colonial days of the 1600s), but it took many years for experts to crack the code and reveal the message:

'REMEMBER DEATH'.

ULTIMATE DEAR JOHN LETTER

The epitaph on the gravestone of John Laird McCaffery in Notre-Dame-de-Neiges cemetery in Montreal reads:

JOHN
FREE YOUR BODY AND SOUL
UNFOLD YOUR WINGS AND FLY
CLIMB THE HIGHEST MOUNTAINS
KICK YOUR FEET UP IN THE AIR
YOU MAY NOW LIVE FOR EVER
OR RETURN TO THIS EARTH
UNLESS YOU FEEL GOOD WHERE YOU ARE!

Nice – unless you read the first letter of each sentence from top to bottom! Apparently the 'acrostic' stone was ordered jointly by the deceased's ex-wife and his mistress.

(*See also* 15. IN SPORT, *Acrostic Brick*; 2. ACCESSORIES, *Acrostic Jewellery*)

28. IN THE GARDEN

The art of floriography, the language of flowers, took root and flourished in the restrained atmosphere of Victorian social life and etiquette.

Floriography is the assignment of meaning to specific flowers in order to convey coded messages that could not otherwise be spoken in public. Messages passed between lovers using a single flower, floral arrangement, even a floral scent on a handkerchief.

How much the code was used is disputed, but the idea was popular and increasingly elaborate. If flowers were offered upside down, for example, their meaning was reversed. Offered with the right hand sometimes meant 'Yes', offered with the left hand they meant 'No'.

There were manuals to help the lovelorn, but they sometimes differed over the meaning of specific flowers. Here are some of the more commonly agreed-upon.

ACACIA	Friendship
ACONITE	Treachery
AMBROSIA	Love returned
BASIL	Hatred
BEGONIA	Beware
BELLADONNA	Silence
BINDWEED	Hope extinguished
BLUEBELL	Constancy, kindness
BUTTERFLY WEED	Let me go
CAMOMILE	Energy in adversity
CANDYTUFT	I'm indifferent
CAPE JASMINE	I'm too happy

CHICKWEED	Rendezvous
COBOEA	Gossip
CURRANTS	Your frown will kill me
CYCLAMEN	Goodbye
DIANTHUS	Make haste
DILL	Lust
EVENING PRIMROSE	Inconstancy
EVERLASTING PEA	Don't go away
FILBERT	Reconciliation
FOUR-LEAVED CLOVER	Be mine
GARDEN DAISY	I share your feelings
GARDEN MARIGOLD	Uneasiness
GLOXINIA	Love at first sight
GRAMMANTHES	Your temper is too hasty
HEART'S EASE	Think of me, I think of you
HELLEBORE	Scandal
HONEY FLOWER, MOTHERWORT, MIMOSA	Secret love
IRIS	I have a message for you
IVY GERANIUM	Your hand for the next dance
JONQUIL	Return my affection
LETTUCE	Cold-heartedness
LOVE IN A MIST	You puzzle me
MAIDEN'S HAIR	Discretion
MARIGOLD	Cruelty, grief, despair
MEADOW SAFFRON	My best days are past
MONKSHOOD	A deadly foe is near
MORNING GLORY	Love in vain

MYRTLE	Love in absence
NARCISSUS	Egotism
NIGHT CONVOLVULUS	Tonight
NUTMEG GERANIUM	I expect a meeting
OLEANDER, RHODODENDRON	Beware
OSMUNDA	I dream of you
PANSY	I think of you
PEA	Appointed meeting
PENNYROYAL	Flee away!
PLUM TREE	Keep your promise
PURPLE HYACINTH	Sorry, please forgive me
RED BALSAM, BURDOCK	Touch me not
RED TULIP	Declaration of love
ROSE GERANIUM	I prefer you
SATIN FLOWER	Am I forgotten?
SHEPHERD'S PURSE	I offer you my all
SINGLE CHINA ASTER	I'll think about it
SNAPDRAGON	You are presumptive, no never
SNOWBALL	Good news
SOLID-COLOURED CARNATION	Yes
SPIDER FLOWER	Elope with me
SPIDERWORT	Esteem, not love
STRIPED CARNATION	No, I can't be with you
SWEET PEA	Departure, good bye
TUBEROSE	Dangerous pleasures
VISCARIA	Will you dance with me?
WHITE CATCHFLY	Betrayed

WHITE CLOVER	I promise
WHITE VERBENA	Pray for me
WILD LICORICE	I declare against you
WILD SORREL	Ill-timed wit
YELLOW CARNATION	Disappointment
YELLOW TULIP	Hopeless love

If you are invited for dinner it is polite to take a gift of flowers for your hostess. But be careful: in Russia, you must bring an odd number of flowers – even numbers are only for funerals.

JUST ROSES

Roses convey a powerful message, from the 'blown rose' in a still life to the rebranding of Labour. Giving someone a red rose means 'I love you'. But check the shade: in floriography, a dark red rose means shame.

During the War of the Roses the symbol of the House of Lancaster was the red rose; the House of York's was the white rose. The Tudor Rose of England deliberately combines the two. In the eighteenth century the white rose was the badge of the Jacobites who sought to restore the Stuarts to the throne.

On 19 May every year a florist visits the church of St Peter ad Vincula in the Tower of London, and lays a basket of red roses on Anne Boleyn's resting-place (a plaque near the altar stands in for her unmarked grave). 19 May marks the anniversary of her execution in 1536. However, nobody knows who orders or pays for the roses, more than 450 years after her death.

(*See also Primroses* and *Edelweiss and the White Rose below*; 22. **IN LITERATURE**, *Edgar Allan Poe*; 18. **ON TELEVISION**, *Ugly Betty and Ann Boleyn*)

■ THE FLORIOGRAPHY OF ROSES

CAMPION	Only deserve my love
CHRISTMAS	Relieve my anxiety
CORAL	Desire
DARK PINK	Thankfulness
DEEP RED	Shame
DOG	Pleasure and pain
FULL-BLOWN	I love you; over two buds: secrecy
JAPAN	Beauty is your only attraction (ouch)
LAVENDER	Enchantment
LEAF	You may hope
MUSK	Your beauty is capricious
ORANGE	Fascination
TEA	I will remember
THORNLESS	Love at first sight
WHITE	I am worthy of you
WHITE DRIED	I'd choose death over loss of virtue
WHITE ROSEBUD	You are/I am too young to love
YELLOW	Infidelity, decrease of love

■ CEILING ROSE

The modern ceiling rose is a direct architectural descendant of the 'sub-rosa' – an ancient secret sign to keep your lips sealed 'under the rose'.

According to the myth the goddess Aphrodite gave a rose to her son Eros. Concerned about his mother's sexual indiscretions, Eros gave it to the god of silence, Harpocrates, to prevent gossip.

At Roman banquets the host hung a rose from the ceiling to indicate that all secrets stayed in the room as they were 'sub-rosa'. In the Middle Ages a rose was painted or carved on the ceiling of council chambers and over confessional boxes, with the same sub-rosa message. American socialite Caroline Astor received guests under the rose medallion in her morning room where all gossip was considered 'sub-rosa'.

MYTH ALERT

The nursery rhyme 'Ring a Ring o' Roses' is code for the Great Plague of the fourteeth century. Symptoms included a rash ('ring of roses') and sneezing ('A-tishoo'). A 'pocketful of posies' was handy for masking the stench and protected you from infection. 'We all fall down' refers to the death of almost a third of the population.

It's a good story. But there is no written evidence of the rhyme before 1881, over 500 years after the event. Could it have survived orally for that long? Also, there are different versions of the words, most of which don't fit the Plague theory.

People did carry around 'pocketfuls of posies' or their equivalent. Judges at the Old Bailey still sometimes carry nosegays of aromatic herbs, a tradition dating back to a time when typhus was endemic in the old Newgate Prison - now the site of The Royal Courts of Justice, including the Old Bailey.

PRIMROSES

In 1881, the same year 'Ring a Ring o' Roses' first appeared, Benjamin Disraeli died. Every year on 19 April, the anniversary of his death, his favourite primroses are placed on his monument in Parliament Square (see above right).

(*See also Just Roses, above* and **22. IN LITERATURE,** *Edgar Allan Poe*)

Floral tributes at Disraeli's statue, 1930

VIOLETS

The violet, the 'little flower that comes back in the spring', was the secret symbol of Napoleon Bonaparte's followers during his exile on Elba in 1814. His nickname was 'Corporal Violet'.

This picture of a bunch of violets (above), from an engraving by Canu in 1815, was circulated among his supporters. It contains the secret profiles of Napoleon, his wife Marie Louise and their three-year-old son Charles. Can you find all three?

EDELWEISS AND THE WHITE ROSE

During the Nazi regime Germany, two youthful anti-Nazi movements were named after flowers.

The 'Edelweiss Pirates' were a loose group of working-class teenagers, numbering up to 5,000, who offered an illegal alternative to Hitler Youth. Initially this involved camping, hanging around, meeting girls. Later they fought against Hitler Youth, painted anti-Nazi graffiti, stole for local resistance groups and carried out acts of sabotage. The 'White Rose Society' was a small group of students at the University of Munich who distributed leaflets calling for active resistance to the Nazis. Many Pirates were executed or sent to concentration camps. The White Rose students were beheaded.

(*See also* 22. **IN LITERATURE** *for Scarlet Pimpernel*)

29. IN THE COUNTRY

DOGGING

Dogging is the practice of having sex in a public place, especially in a car. It was made even more public by the activities of a former Nottingham Forest, Liverpool and England striker in Cannock Chase, Staffordshire.

Why 'dogging'? Perhaps because couples are 'dogged' or 'pursued' by voyeurs. Or from a common excuse for being in the woods at night: 'I was walking the dog'. It may even refer to having uninhibited sex like dogs: outside, in public and with strangers. No one really knows.

There are three sets of people involved: the couple having sex in the car, the people watching the couple (the voyeurs), and the voyeurs who join in with the couple. To manage this between strangers, a system of secret signs evolved:

- **FLASH** (interior and exterior) **CAR LIGHTS** = we are doggers
- **LEAVE INTERIOR LIGHT ON** = we want to be watched
- **LOWER WINDOW A BIT** = get closer or join in for oral sex (through the window)
- **LOWER WINDOW FULLY** = we want to be fondled
- **OPEN CAR DOOR** = come and join in

Dogging events are largely organised on the internet (where else?). Some doggers also put a sticker or picture of a dog in the rear window, as a secret sign to other doggers (*See also* **36. ON A CAR,** *Accessories*).

Doggers may also signal an interest in 'carping' (talking to strangers on the phone while pleasuring yourself privately or publicly by writing their phone number on a card and displaying it inside the car.

Remember, dogging may be illegal where you live, and carries sizeable risk as it involves sex with strangers and assumes that everyone will behave safely.

THREE

For outdoorsy people, '3' is the most common distress signal. It maybe three gunshots, blasts of a whistle or a horn, or smoke signals. Seen from the air, three rocks, fires or other markings positioned in a triangle also say 'Help'.

However, the official international distress call is six blasts, rocks etc. with three being an acknowledgement that your signal has been received and understood.

SMOKE

To make a smoke signal, individual puffs of smoke are created by lighting a fire and then periodically covering it with a blanket.

Smoke signals were essentially a private system of communication between tribe members, indicating, for example, that a battle was won or lost, or that there was sickness at the camp. About the only common signals were:

- **'ONE PUFF'** – Attention
- **'TWO PUFFS'** – All's well
- **'THREE PUFFS'** – Danger, trouble, help

The main advantage of smoke was the distance it could be seen at and the relaying of the message. Soldiers on the Great Wall of China could send a message from tower to tower over 300 miles in just a few hours.

The most famous smoke signal is when the College of Cardinals is locked in the Sistine Chapel to choose a new Pope. When they have decided, white smoke emerges from the chimney. If they can't reach a decision, black smoke is the signal. This doesn't always work and can cause great confusion!

TRAIL SIGNS

Trail signs are made by someone marking a trail for another to follow, preferably with natural resources to hand (twigs, stones, grass), and are visible on the ground on the left-hand side of the trail.

You can spot the trail's direction from an arrow made from three twigs laid on the ground, a twig stuck in the ground at an acute angle, an arrow of small stones, one Y-shaped twig pointing through another or a small rock atop a bigger one.

The distance may be shown using twigs like this:

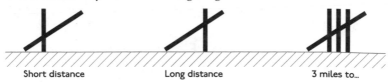

Short distance   Long distance   3 miles to...

A cross of twigs, stones or chalk means 'Don't follow this trail'. If the direction of the trail changes you may find clumps of grass or a bush bent left or right, or stones laid out like this:

Turn left   Turn right

A dot within a circle means 'I've gone home'. This trail sign is engraved on the headstone of Lord Baden-Powell, founder of the Scout movement, who is buried in Nyeri in Kenya. See opposite.

(*See also* 1. **MEETING**, *Scouts*; 13. **IN ESPIONAGE**, *Baden-Powell*)

Lord Baden Powell's grave

BLAZING

Blazing is the marking of a trail (literally 'trail-blazing') with directional markers called 'blazes'. Originally it was done by carving arrows and other symbols into the bark of trees.

Nowadays, blazes are created by scraping away a small rectangle of outer bark (about the size of a £5 note) and painting it in. Different colours are used, but blue is common as it is one of the least natural colours in a forest.

You usually find blazes just above head height, and within line of the sight of each other.

North American blaze system

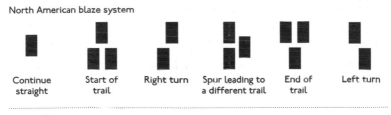

| Continue straight | Start of trail | Right turn | Spur leading to a different trail | End of trail | Left turn |

HASH MARKS

The Hash House Harriers are an international running club that organises social non-competitive runs similar to hare and hounds. One 'hare' lays a trail for the rest of the 'hounds' to follow. Unlike professional athletes, HHH's motto is 'a drinking club with a running problem'.

It began in 1938 in Kuala Lumpur when a group of British colonials started hare and hounds runs on a Monday evening to work off their weekend hangovers. There are now clubs or 'kennels' all over the world and you may see their temporary signs in the country and the city.

Hashing has its own blazing system. The 'hare' lays a trail with a series of clues using flour, chalk, potting soil or toilet paper (in 2007 a flour trail in Connecticut triggered an anthrax alert). Trails include false trails (falsies) to trick the hounds. Once he finds the true trail, the hound calls 'On-On' to alert the rest of the pack. Events conclude with social drinking, called an 'On-On-On' or 'On-After'.

■ HASH MARKS

●	**HASH MARK**	Trail here. 3 hash marks in a row indicates true trail
⧎	**HARE ARROW**	Arrow laid only by a hare. A hare arrow always indicates the true trail
⊗	**CHECK**	Trail may change direction. Hounds must search for true trail and ignore any 'falsies'
⊙⊙	**BOOB CHECK**	'Check' as above, but only a woman must find the true trail.

≡	**FALSE TRAIL**	False trail. Go back to last 'check' to look for true trail
Ⓑ	**BEER NEAR**	Beer stop close by
Ⓡ	**REGROUP**	FRBs (Front Running Bastards) wait here until the pack regroups and DFL (Dead Fucking Last) hound arrives
T↖↗E ⅄	**TRAIL SPLITS**	Trail splits into two routes: easy (turkey) and difficult (eagle). They will join up eventually
ON IN	**NEARLY THERE**	You've nearly reached the end of the trail

HASHES TO HASHES

In January 2008, a few days after 84-year-old Stevie Wood was cremated, her daughter Sandy and son-in-law Geoff mixed her ashes with flour, and used them to mark a five-mile trail through the Dorset countryside.

The 'Stevie Wood Memorial Hash' was organised by the Hardy Hash House Harriers, of which Geoff is the secretary, and finished in the local pub.

WEATHER SIGNS

When you're out in the country, you can outwit the weatherman by making your own forecasts – if you know the signs.

The most common weather saying is probably 'Red sky at night, shepherd's delight, red sky in the morning, shepherd's warning'. Surprisingly, this is in the Bible (Matthew 16:2-3) when the Pharisees ask Jesus to show them a sign from heaven. Jesus replies:

> *When it is evening, you say, 'It will be fair weather, for the*

sky is red.' And in the morning, 'It will be stormy today, for the sky is red and threatening.' You know how to interpret the appearance of the sky, but you cannot interpret the signs of the times.

By all accounts, this sign is fairly accurate: a red sky at night means the setting sun is shining through an atmosphere of dust particles, which indicates high pressure and stable air coming from the West, which suggests good weather on the way.

Here are some more signs to look for in the country:

If the birds fly low,
Expect rain and a blow

Swallows and bats prefer to fly in dense air, because they get greater lift with their wings. In low-pressure (bad) weather they fly low to the ground, in high-pressure (good) weather, they fly high. You may also see seagulls sitting on the beach rather than soaring above.

Low pressure also seems to affect cows, who lie down rather than go to pasture. Flying insects become more active and fly closer to the ground. If the humidity is high, cicadas go silent because they can't vibrate their wings.

When the weather is dry and humidity is low, spiders tend to

spin bigger and thicker webs, and cats groom themselves more, to moisten their fur and get rid of static electricity.

When leaves turn their back
'Tis a sign it's going to rain

Several plants fold up their petals before rain, including tulips, dandelions, bindweed, and chickweed. Oak and maple trees curl up their leaves. Marshes or swamp land tend to pong more strongly, as the low pressure causes them to release more methane from their murky depths.

When clouds appear like rocks and towers,
The earth's refreshed with frequent showers

Cumulonimbus clouds occur when moist warm air rises and can cause heavy showers, usually quite brief. Moist warm air also makes your wooden garden furniture squeak.

If you want to know how warm it is, listen to the crickets. Count the number of times they chirp in 15 seconds, and add 37. That will give a rough temperature in Fahrenheit. To find out how cold it is, look at the rhododendrons: the colder it is the more their leaves curl up and hang down. They are only fully open at about 15°C.

30. AT THE PALACE

FLAG SIGNALS

The Queen's official flag is not the Union Jack but the Royal Standard, flown when she is in residence in one of the royal palaces. If the Union Jack (or in Scotland the Royal Standard of the King of Scots) is flying above the building, the Queen is not in residence.

The Royal Standard is never flown at half mast, even after the death of a monarch, because there is always a sovereign on the throne ('the King is dead, long live the King'). This fact was lost on the press and public when Diana, Princess of Wales, died and the Royal Family was lambasted for not flying the Queen's flag on top of Buckingham Palace at half-mast.

GUARDS

To tell which regiment is guarding the Queen today, here are the signs:

	HEADGEAR	PLUME	PLUME COLOUR	BUTTON SPACING	TUNIC
LIFE GUARDS	METAL HELMET	ON HELMET	WHITE	(METAL BREASTPLATE)	RED
BLUES & ROYALS	METAL HELMET	ON HELMET	RED	(METAL BREASTPLATE)	RED
GRENADIER	BEARSKIN	ON LEFT	WHITE	SINGLY	BLUE
COLDSTREAM	BEARSKIN	ON RIGHT	RED	PAIRS	RED
SCOTS	BEARSKIN	NO PLUME	–	THREES	RED
IRISH	BEARSKIN	ON RIGHT	BLUE	FOURS	RED
WELSH	BEARSKIN	ON LEFT	WHITE/GREEN WHITE	FIVES	RED

GUN SALUTES

The standard Royal gun salute is 21 rounds (odd numbers are considered lucky, except 13). If you are visiting the Tower of London on a Royal anniversary, take ear plugs. They fire 62 rounds: 21 as above, plus 20 because the Tower is a Royal Palace, and another 21 for the 'City of London'.

SPOT THE QUEEN

The Queen wears blocks of one colour and distinctive hats so she can be easily spotted by crowds of well-wishers.

Her personal bonnet mascot – a solid-silver figure of St George slaying the dragon – is attached to whichever vehicle she is travelling in. On official business the Queen's Rolls, Bentley and other cars have no number plate.

HANDBAG CODE

If the Queen puts her handbag on the table top she would like the event to end in about five minutes. If she puts it on the floor she wants to be rescued and a lady-in-waiting will shortly appear. If it is hanging from the crook of her left arm, she is fine. On walkabouts, she holds her handbag to one side to show she intends to move on, at which point a lady-in-waiting joins the conversation, allowing HM to slip away without causing offence.

TEATIME

Apparently the Queen is only served rounded sandwiches; according to the tradition anybody serving the Monarch food with pointed edges is attempting to overthrow them.

DEBS' DELIGHT CODE

Until 1958 young upper-class ladies were introduced at Court at the beginning of the social season. The 'Debutantes' were presented to the reigning monarch, and then spent the evening in the company of 'suitable' bachelors: the 'Debs' Delights'. To discuss the merits of the men privately, the ladies used the Debs' Delight code, e.g.

FI	Financially insecure
HD	Heavy drinker
MTF	Must touch flesh
MSC	Makes skin crawl
NQOCD	Not quite our class, dear
NSIT	Not safe in taxis
TPF	Tiny prying fingers
VVSITPQ	Very very safe in taxis, probably queer

Queen Elizabeth II abolished the Court presentation in 1958.

COAT OF ARMS

For his eighteenth birthday Prince William received a new coat of arms from the Queen. Hidden within it is a red scallop shell. This is to commemorate his mother, Diana, whose family the Spencers have had the pilgrim shell on their arms since the sixteenth century.

There are three more scallop shells to find, on the necks of three animals: the lion on the crest, the supporting lion and the supporting unicorn. (*See also* 2. **ACCESSORIES**, *Scallop Shell*)

The arms of the late Queen Mother contained bows and lions, a pun on her family name, Bowes-Lyons. The arms of her great-granddaughter Princess Beatrice have three bees (bees thrice).

(*See also* 31. **IN A COAT OF ARMS**)

31. IN A COAT OF ARMS

Heraldry has been called 'the shorthand of history'. The many different colours, shapes, animals, positioning and shield divisions represent events in the family history, honours bestowed by royalty, achievements in the battlefield, puns on the family name, and much more.

For example, Winston Churchill, John Wesley and the Spencers have scallop shells on their arms, often a sign that an ancestor made the pilgrimage to the shrine of St James at Santiago de Compostella. Arms within a lozenge belong to a woman (being non-combatant, women didn't need shields). Thistles or dirks indicate a Scottish connection.

Heraldry comes from a time when knights wore armour and you couldn't tell who was who on the battlefield or in a tournament. A 'coat of arms' was literally the surcoat worn over your armour with your mark or design upon it.

You can sometimes work out which family a coat of arms belongs to if it contains 'canting': a visual pun on their name. For example the arms of the only English Pope, Adrian IV, include a broken spear. His name was Nicholas Breakspear. The arms of Bartolomeo Colleoni (1400-75), an Italian soldier of fortune bears three testicles, a pun on his name (*coglione* = testicle).

(*See also* 30. **AT THE PALACE** *for the Canting Arms of Queen Mother and Princess Beatrice*)

In 2004 Beatles producer Sir George Martin was granted a coat of arms filled with canting. On the crest, a House Martin holds a recorder. On the shield are three stag beetles, separated by five parallel lines representing musical staves, and/or guitar strings. The motto translates roughly as 'All you Need is Love'.

The left-hand medal is that of the Knight Bachelor, the right

Commander of the British Empire (CBE).

The zebra holding an abbot's crozier is a reference to the zebra crossing on the Abbey Road album. The people who believe this album cover is code for 'Paul McCartney is dead' point to the fact that there are only 3 beetles on Martin's coat of arms.

(*See also* 32. **IN MUSIC,** *Album covers, The Beatles / Abbey Road*; 2. **ACCESSORIES,** *Scallop Shell*).

32. IN MUSIC

ALBUM COVERS

■ **MARILYN MANSON/MECHANICAL ANIMALS** This controversial album from Marilyn Manson (né Brian Warner) contains a number of secret signs.

Released in September 1998 it features Manson in the dual roles of himself ('Alpha'), and an androgynous alien not unlike Bowie's *Ziggy Stardust* ('Omega'). The vinyl version came in separate albums: an opaque white LP credited to Manson, and a transparent blue LP credited to Omega and the Mechanical Animals. The booklet contained hidden messages you could only read by viewing it through the original blue CD packaging, or the transparent blue LP.

- I no longer knew if Coma White was real or just a side effect
- Now children it's time for recess, please roll up your sleeves
- Even machines can see that we are dead

Another secret sign is '15' which appears in various forms throughout the album. Manson's birthday is 5 January or 1/5 in American date format. The album was released on 15 September. On the cover his name is spelt MAR1LYN MAN5ON. One of the tracks is called 'New Model No. 15'. On the CD only there are 15 tracks, of which one is hidden and playable only on a computer. Omega has 15 computer keys on his forehead.

Mechanical Animals was the top-selling album in the week of its release. The following April during the album tour, two students shot a teacher and 12 students at Columbine High School in Colorado, and a media frenzy blaming Manson's music and lyrics for influencing the killers followed. Manson cancelled the rest of tour and issued a statement describing the massacre as 'tragic and disgusting'.

ROGER DEAN/YES

Artist Roger Dean is well known for his fantasy landscapes, and for his association with the band YES, for whom he designed many album covers.

In *Tales from Topographic Oceans* (1973) the constellations in the sky are the astrological signs of each band member: Aries (Steve Howe), Scorpio (Jon Anderson), Gemini (Alan White), Pisces (Chris Squire), Taurus (Rick Wakeman). The 1974 tour of the album is said to have inspired *This is Spinal Tap* (1984).

PINK FLOYD/THE FINAL CUT

The coloured stripes on the cover of *The Final Cut* (1983) are service medal ribbons from WW2:

Black and red stripes on yellow-green background	Defence Medal for three years' service
Black, red and blue stripes on gold background	Africa Star, for service in North African campaign
Red stripe on blue	1939–45 Star, for at least 6 months' service 1939–45
White and purple diagonal stripes	Distinguished Flying Cross: Awarded to officers 'for acts of courage, valour or devotion to duty while flying'

PET SHOP BOYS/INTEGRAL

In 2007 the Pet Shop Boys released their remix album *Disco Four*. A single from that album, 'Integral', was released in a download-only format. The cover artwork is in QR code – a two-dimensional bar code popular in Japan.

QR stands for Quick Response. The code can be printed physically (on ads, business cards, in magazines etc.) and then scanned by anybody with a camera phone and the right software, to provide a hard link to a specific URL. (*See example left*)

The QR code on 'Integral' gives a link to the Pet Shop Boys website.

■ ROGER WATERS/RADIO KAOS

The cover of Radio KAOS features Morse code which translates (more or less) as the names of the artist, album and the tracks:

ROGER WATERS RADIO KAOS WHO NEEDS INFORMATION THE POWERS THAT BE HOME THE TIDE IS TURNING RADIO WAVES

Morse at the beginning and end of the album supposedly contains a verse from 'The Tide is Turning', deleted to avoid legal complications because it is critical of Sylvester Stallone and the *Rambo* films of the time:

> We will not be dragged down into his South China sea of macho bullshit and mediocrity.

The track 'Perfect Sense', apparently includes a back-masked message critical of Stanley Kubrick. The story goes that Waters asked Kubrick if he could use breathing sounds from *2001: A Space Odyssey*. When Kubrick said no, Waters recorded his own breathing sounds as well as the message.

(*See Back-masking and Morse Alert below*)

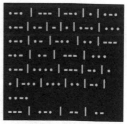

A re-production of the album cover

■ TAKING BACK SUNDAY/TELL ALL YOUR FRIENDS

This American band put the number 152 on their album artwork to remember where they came from and to let their friends back home know they haven't forgotten them.

Lead singer Adam Lazzara is from High Point in North Carolina. When he and his friends travelled from there along Highway 40 to Chapel Hill to see shows, they would always stop at Exit 152. This exit appears on their debut album *Tell All Your Friends* (2002), and the number 152 is somewhere every album to date.

■ THE BEATLES/ABBEY ROAD

Triggered by a hoax by DJ Russell Gibb, *Abbey Road* (1969) was believed by many fans to contain secret signs that Paul McCartney was dead:

- Paul is barefoot, eyes closed, out of step, and with a cigarette in his right hand even though he is left-handed
- The VW's number plate is LMW 281F. LMW is said to stand for 'Linda my wife', or 'Linda McCartney Weeps'
- '28' meant Paul would have been 28 if he were still alive

The four Beatles supposedly represent:

- **THE PRIEST** (John, dressed in white)
- **THE UNDERTAKER** (Ringo in a black suit)
- **THE CORPSE** (Paul, in a suit but barefoot – like a body in a casket)
- **THE GRAVEDIGGER** (George, in jeans and a work shirt).

The earlier Beatle track 'Revolution 9' on the *White Album* (1968) also fed the rumour. Played backwards it seemed to repeat 'Turn me on, dead man ('number nine' played forwards), 'Let me out!' and 'There were two, there are none now' while the background sound collage was supposedly Paul's fatal car accident.

(*See Back-Masking below*)

WHITE STRIPES

Jack White, of the band White Stripes, trained as a furniture upholsterer. In an interview Jack revealed how he secretly upholstered poetry inside whichever chair he was working on at the time. It's presumably still there.

BACK-MASKING

Back-masking is a recording technique where a message is hidden on a music track by recording it backwards onto the track and then playing it forwards.

In the Beatles album *Revolver* (1966) the track 'Rain' contains the back-masked message: 'Sunshine... Rain... When the rain comes, they run and hide their heads'. The Queen track 'Another One Bites the Dust' allegedly contains the line 'It's fun to smoke marijuana' when played backwards.

There has been a persistent accusation since the 1980s that some rock albums deliberately contain back-masked Satanic messages. Far-right Christian groups in the US say the devil is known to practice 'the backward expression of messages' (the Lord's Prayer and all that) and therefore is bound to do so in rock music.

In 1981, rock band Styx was accused of putting a satanic message in the opening verse of 'Snowblind', a song about cocaine addiction. When the line 'I try so hard to make it so' is played backwards, it is said to say 'Satan move through our voices'. In 1990 the band Judas Priest was sued by the parents of two young men who attempted a suicide pact with a shot to the head (one succeeded). The unsuccessful civil case argued that the men had been influenced by a back-masked message 'Do it, do it' on a track from their 1978 album *Stained Class*, along with the disturbing cover. However, there is no hard evidence that subliminal messages in music have any effect. Many so-called messages are hard to make out and open to interpretation. Experiments have shown that if you've been told what to hear, you tend to hear it whether it's actually there or not.

Most recently, the TV series *Lost* included a back-masked message in Season 3:7 as part of its plethora of hidden clues:

Only fools are enslaved by time and space

More recent back-masked messages either parody the Satanism controversy or are audio 'Easter eggs' for fans.

E.L.O.	Fire on High	The music is reversible, but time is not...turn back! turn back! turn back!
INFORMATION SOCIETY	Are Friends Electric?	Obey your parents. Do your homework. Winners don't do drugs.
OZZY OSBOURNE	Bloodbath in Paradise	Your mothers sell whelks in Hull (a parody of the line from *The Exorcist*: 'Your mother sucks c**ks in hell')
PETRA	Judas Kiss	What are you looking for the devil for, when you ought to be looking for the Lord?
PINK FLOYD	Empty Spaces	Hello hunters. Congratulations. You've just discovered the secret message...
PRINCE	Darling Nikki	Hello, how are you? I'm fine cos I know that the Lord is coming soon...
WEIRD AL YANKOVIC	Nature Trail to Hell	Satan eats Cheese Whizz

What happens when you play a country music record backwards? You get your girl back, you get your truck back, you get your dog back...

(*See also* I. **MEETING**, *Judas Kiss*)

BAND NAMES

Some bands choose their name by sticking a pin in a map (e.g. Bay City Rollers), other a finger in a dictionary (e.g. The Commodores). Many are named after porn film titles, sex toys, comics, horror films, Nazism, drugs, slang words for penis, and unemployment. A remarkable number originate from William Burroughs (e.g. Steely Dan, Soft Machine, and the phrase 'heavy metal').

10CC	After a dream by disgraced pop promo Jonathan King, not as rumoured after the average amount of sperm in a male ejaculation (more like 3cc, chaps!). King also named Genesis.
311	Omaha police code for indecent exposure, after band members were arrested for skinny-dipping in a public pool. Nothing to do with the KKK.
DOOBIE BROTHERS	A 'doobie' was slang for a marijuana joint in California.
FOO FIGHTERS	US Air Force slang for alien-looking fireballs seen over Germany in WW2.
GREEN DAY	A 'green day' is one when you just sit about smoking pot.
JOY DIVISION	Line of huts in a concentration camp lived in by female prisoners forced to sleep with Nazi officers.
KING CRIMSON	Synonym for Beelzebub.
LYNYRD SKYNYRD	After gym teacher Leonard Skinner whom the boys disliked at high school.
'N SYNC	Last letter of original band members' names: Justin (Timberlake), Chris, Joey, Jason and JC. Jason Gallasso was replaced by Lance Bass.
POGUES	From 'Pogue Mahone', Irish Gaelic for 'kiss my ass'.

| SCISSOR SISTERS | 'Scissor' is a sexual position where two women face each other crotch to crotch. Of the four male members (!) three are openly gay, the only female member is not. |

SINGER NAMES

BONO	Real name Paul Hewson, named after a hearing-aid store in Dublin called Bonovox, Latin for 'good voice'.
EMINEM	From his initials Marshall Mathers III. He originally performed under the name M&M.
MOBY	Nicknamed (by his parents) after his great-great-great-great uncle Herman Melville, author of classic novel *Moby-Dick* (1851). His real name is Richard Melville Hall.
JELLY ROLL MORTON	'Jelly Roll' is slang for penis. Morton was a jazz musician and a pimp. Ice T took his name from legendary pimp Iceberg Slim.
GARY NUMAN	Picked 'Numan' out of the listing for a plumbing company in the Yellow Pages.
PRINCE	From 1993-2000 Prince named himself after the unpronounceable title of his fourteenth album.
STING	Real name Gordon Sumner, named after the yellow and black striped shirt he used to wear, that made him look like a bee.

ENIGMA VARIATIONS

Seated at the piano one day in 1898, Sir Edward Elgar (1857-1934) idly composed a short melody. Encouraged by his wife Caroline, he then devised a series of variations on the theme, each of which was a musical portrait of one of their friends.

So which variation matches which friend? Elgar put clues in the score, using nicknames or initials. So for example, Variation 1 refers to his wife, as it repeats a short 4-note melody Elgar whistled whenever he got home. Variation 10 uses the woodwind to reprise the stutter or laugh of their friend Dora Penny.

Below the main theme Elgar hid a second, of which he said: 'through and over the whole set another and larger theme "goes", but is not played... even as in some late dramas ... the chief character is never on stage'.

Various solutions have been suggested, from 'God Save the Queen' to 'Auld Land Syne'. Another contender is 1 Corinthians, 13:12:

> *For now we see through a glass, darkly but then face to face:*
> *now I know in part; but then shall I know even as also*
> *I am known.*

because in the Latin Vulgate Bible, 'darkly' is written 'in enigmate'.

MOTIFS IN MUSIC

Elgar was following a long tradition of composers putting musical ciphers into their work. In the eighteenth and nineteenth centuries, Schumann, Brahms and Bach all used musical notation itself to spell out names or phrases.

The most commonly used notation is 'French', where notes are represented on five-line staves by the letters A to G. One of Brahms' friends, a violinist called Joseph Joachim (right), used this notation to create his own motif. For him, the three-note phrase F-A-E stood for 'Frei Aber Einsam', free but lonely. In his Third Symphony, Brahms challenged this sad motif with one of his own: F-A-F, 'Frei Aber Froh', free but happy.

In 'German' notation, the letter B is used to represent B-flat (as it was used the most) and H stands for B-natural. This allowed Bach to spell out his own surname as a musical motif, B-A-C-H.

Liszt, Rimsky-Korsakov and others paid homage to Bach by using his B-A-C-H motif in their own work.

Another musical notation is 'Do-Re-Mi', as in *The Sound of Music* (1965). Shostakovich mixed German and French notation with Do-Re-Mi to spell out his own initials, D-S-C-H (above), as well as his lover Elmira's: E La Mi Re A.

More recently, John Williams slipped a three-note motif from the score for *Psycho* (1960) into the score for *Star Wars* (1977) as a homage to composer Bernard Herrmann.

MORSE ALERT

Aside from TV and movie themes there is a surprising amount of Morse hidden in popular music.

Like progressive rock band Dream Theater: the track 'In the Name of God' on their album *Train of Thought* (2003–4) contains the message 'Eat my ass and balls' in Morse code. No doubt metal fans have also spotted that the band's logo is based on the mark of Mary Queen of Scots! Mary herself used codes and ciphers to communicate with her allies while a prisoner.

Moving Pictures (1981), the album from Canadian rock band Rush, includes the track 'YYZ'. In Morse this is the transmitter code for the Lester B. Pearson International Airport in Toronto. The code -·-- -·-- --·· (YYZ) forms the rhythm underlying most of the song.

In 1967 psychedelic folk band Pearls Before Swine released a song called '(Oh Dear) Miss Morse'. In the chorus the band sing:

Dit Dit Dah Dit / Dit Dit Dah / Dah Dit Dah Dit / Dah Dit Dah

As they sing each line, the Morse is tapped out as well:

F ··-· / U ··- / C -·-· / K -·-

It was banned from the radio after ex-servicemen and scoutmasters rang in to complain.

33. OVERHEARD

RHYMING SLANG

Many people think rhyming slang evolved as a 'secret language' designed by Cockneys to prevent the Old Bill or the punter at your market stall from understanding what you were saying. Some historians, however, think this theory is a load of Watford (Gap).

Whatever the case it is surprising how often we use this code without realising it. Have a butcher's at this:

Barnet	**BARNET FAIR**	Hair
Doing 'bird'	**BIRDLIME**	Time
Bread	**BREAD AND HONEY**	Money
Gone for a Burton	**BURTON-ON-TRENT**	Went
Have a butcher's	**BUTCHER'S HOOK**	Look
Cobblers	**COBBLER'S AWLS**	Balls
Use your loaf	**LOAF OF BREAD**	Head
Take the Mickey	**MICKEY BLISS**	Piss
Tell porkies	**PORK PIES**	Lies
Raspberry	**RASPBERRY TART**	Fart
The Sweeney	**SWEENEY TODD**	Flying Squad

A cobbler's awl, one of a pair

REVERSE SLANG

Another way to hide the meaning of a word is to turn it around. For example, in Tic-Tac the word 'roof' means '4-1' i.e. 'four' backwards. We also use reverse-slang in everyday speech. 'Yob' comes from 'boy' in reverse. We get the word 'bonk' from reversing 'knob' (slang for penis)

The upper class had their own word code, lapsing into French when what they had to say was regarded as 'pas devant les domestiques', or 'pas devant les enfants'. Kids would get their own back using 'pig Latin'. (*See also* 15. **IN SPORT**, *Tic-Tac*)

WHITE LIES

When a particular medical consultant says to his nurse, 'Would you see if Mrs Brown is waiting?' he is actually asking her to get rid of his current patient and bring him a cup of coffee. Like many white lies, the purpose is to avoid being rude. (*See also* 40. **IN HOSPITAL**)

STRAWBERRY FILTER

When TV directors tell their camera operator to 'use the strawberry filter' they mean 'just pretend to be filming this'. It may be that they've got what they need by now, or because the interviewee is so boring it'll be cut anyway. Also known as the 'B-Roll'.

When the equipment fails to work, crews may wonder aloud if the FNG (f**king new guy) has got the DFO (dumb f**king operator) switch on. In the States, TV crew vernacular for Vox Pops, street interviews with the public, is 'AAA' (ask any asshole).

PEBKAC

'I think it's a PEBKAC' is an IT customer support code meaning 'Problem Exists Between Keyboard and Chair': the customer's the problem, not the hardware or software. Sometimes said as PICNIC ('problem in chair not in computer'). If IT tell you it was an 'ID-10-T error', they mean you're an idiot. If they say it must be a 'Layer 8'

problem, the 'Layer 8' is the user. Or 'luser' (user + loser). You.
(*See also* 34. **ON A COMPUTER OR MOBILE**)

POLARI

Polari is a secret language used by sections of the gay community in
Britain between 1900 and the 1970s. It came to popular notice used by
the characters Julian and Sandy in the radio show *Round the Horne*.

Polari is based on slang words from different sources, from
rhyming slang and backslang to Yiddish and Italian. Originally used
around the docks, it was picked up by merchant seamen and later
used in gay pubs and the theatre. After the 1967 Sexual Offences
Act legalised homosexual activity, Polari declined. It has resurfaced
recently in the stage version of *Round the Horne*, and in BBC
comedy *Little Britain*. For example, the only gay in the village
Daffyd was asked by his new gay hairdresser to 'rest his lallies'.

Like rhyming and reverse slang we use Polari words commonly
without being aware of their origins. Khazi or Carsey (toilet) is a
Polari word from the Italian 'casa' meaning house or cottage (hence
the verb 'to cottage'). The word 'camp' supposedly comes from
KAMP, an acronym for Known as Male Prostitute.

BATTS	Shoes	LALLIES	Legs
BIJOU	Small	LILLS	Hands
BONA	Good	LILLY	Police
BUTCH	Masculine	NANTI	Not, no
CAPELLO	Hat	NISHTA	Nothing, no
COD	Naff	OGLEFAKES	Glasses
ECAF or EEK	Face	OMI	Man
FANTABULOSA	Wonderful	OMI-POLONE	Effeminate man
GLOSSIES	Magazines	PALARE PIPE	Telephone
HOOFER	Dancer	SCARPER	Run off

SHIBBOLETHS

A Shibboleth is the use of language or pronunciation to identify people outside your own region, country, group, class, age etc. The word comes from the Bible, Judges 12. To prevent the defeated Ephraimites from returning to their own land across the river Jordan, the Gileadites asked each refugee a simple question:

> *Say now Shibboleth: and he said Shibboleth: for he could not frame to pronounce it right. Then they took him and slew him at the passages of Jordan: and there fell at that time of the Ephraimites forty and two thousand.*

Shibboleths can be useful signs to help you distinguish between different nationalities. For example, Americans pronounce the letter Z as 'zee', whereas Canadians tend to say 'zed'. Aussies say 'fish and chips' like the British, while Kiwis sound more like 'fush and chups' – especially to Aussies.

A shibboleth may indicate whether you are a local or an outsider. For example, natives of San Francisco call their city SF or 'The City', whereas tourists call it San Fran or Frisco. Apparently only visitors call Los Angeles 'LA'. Foreign visitors to Britain regularly mispronounce Edinburgh, Beaulieu and Worcester. Londoners talk about 'the' Edgware Road and 'the' Harrow Road.

Dropping the 'g' from the end of words like 'hunting', 'shooting' and 'fishing' is either working-class or deliberate upper-class mimicry of the working class, but definitely not middle-class. In Northern Ireland it is said that the letter 'H' is pronounced 'Haitch' by Catholics and 'Aitch' by Protestants.

(For wartime shibboleths, see 5. **IN WARTIME**).

34. ON A COMPUTER OR MOBILE

CHAT JARGON

The jargon of chat rooms and text messaging is a mixture of letters, numbers and symbols – from sound-alike (4Q) and metonyms (459), to emoticons (☺) and hippy-speak (420).

Some are decipherable, like BRB (be right back), J/K (just kidding), <3 (love) or even the ironic AFZ (acronym-free zone). But generally the more secret the intent, the more baffling the jargon. This list is 4YEO (for your eyes only):

AMRMTYFTS	All my room mates thank you for the show
A/S/L/P	Age/Sex/Location/Picture
BJJDI	Billy Joel just drove in (someone's swearing a lot)
BOBFOC	Body off Baywatch, Face off Crimewatch
CD9	Code 9 (parents around) Also: P999, MOS (mum over shoulder), PAW (parents are watching), AITR (adults in the room)
CICYHW	Can I copy your homework?
CTC	Choking the chicken (acronym of a euphemism for masturbation)
DILLIGAS	Do I look like I give a shit?
FOL	Fond of leather
IMEZRU	I'm easy, are you
IPN	I'm posting naked
IWSN	I want sex now

KPC	Keeping parents clueless
LMIRL	Let's meet in real life
LOL	Funny (laugh out loud)
NIFOC	Naked in front of computer
NSFW	Not safe for work
OTTOMH	Off the top of my head
ROFL	Rolling on floor laughing
SLAP	Sounds like a plan
TDTM	Talk dirty to me
WUU2	What you up to? (> NM, not much)
X-I-10	Exciting
4Q	F**k you (in a nice way)
8	Oral sex (ate)
143	I love you (1 letter in 'I', 4 letters in 'love', 3 letters in 'you')
159	I love you (phone keys pressed to text ILY)
182	I hate you (eye eight two)
404	Haven't a clue

W00T

In 2007, w00t (spelt with two capital zeroes) was named 'Word of the Year' by Merriam-Webster, the US dictionary. It is gamer/internet slang for 'hooray', and expresses joy, like 'yay'.

PLOKTA

When your computer freezes or otherwise responds incorrectly, you may have tried everything including the '3-Finger Salute' (Control-Alt-Delete) to make it work. In the end you mash lots of keys down at the same time in the vain hope of solving the problem (or easing your frustration). This is known as entering 'plokta' mode, an acronym for Press Lots of Keys to Abort.

PREDICTIVE SLANG

How come teenagers say 'book' when they mean 'cool'? Predictive slang is when you replace a word with the first alternative that comes up when typing a message on your mobile:

TEXT	MEANS	TEXT	MEANS
ADDS	Beer	HONGU	Innit
ANY	Boy	GOOD	Home
BARKING	Carling	HOUR	Hots
BOMB	Anna	LAIDS	Lager
BOOK	Cool	LIPS	Kiss
BRUSH	Crush	NUN	Mum
CAR	Bar	POISONED	Smirnoff
CARNAGE	Barmaid	SHOT	Pint
CASE	Barf	SUB	Pub
CUFF	Buff	ZONINO	Woohoo
EAT	Fat		

RING TONES

In the early twentieth century, most domestic telephones were wired into a 'party line' configuration. All the phones rang at the same time, regardless of who the call was for. To signal who should pick up, each home on the party line was assigned its own ring pattern, like Morse code (e.g. two short rings, followed by one long one). This didn't stop eavesdroppers from listening in!

On Nokia and other phones today, the SMS alert is actually Morse Code for SMS (··· – – ···). Nokia's 'Ascending' SMS alert is Morse for 'Connecting People', the company slogan.

PASSWORDS

The most common computer password is 'password'. Other

top favourites are admin, 123456, qwerty, abc123, monkey, your mother's maiden name, your children's names, your pet's name or your favourite football team. If this sounds too familiar, go and change it now!

@

Before computers, the humble 'at' sign was used in accounting to mean 'at the rate of' e.g. five pears @ 30p each cost £1.50.

However, the symbol's history is far older. Before the printing press, books had to be copied by hand and monks looked for ways to cut down the number of pen strokes per word. Accordingly the word 'ad' was reduced to '@'. According to one theory, it was an abbreviation for 'amphora', a large terracotta jar used to hold wine, spices and other traded goods, and came to be the unit of measurement for the weight and volume held by 1 amphora.

We call the '@' symbol 'at', but it has other more descriptive names in different languages, including the nipple, whirlpool, cinnamon bun, strudel, roll mop, snail, cat's, pig's or monkey's tail, elephant's trunk, little dog, worm and duckling.

In 2007, a report said that a Chinese couple had tried to name their new baby '@', on the basis that it sounds like 'ai ta' or 'love him' in Mandarin.

WEBDINGS

When Microsoft developed Webdings, the graphical font, in 1997, there was a deliberate decision regarding the font and New York City. If you type NYC in Webdings, you get Eye-Heart-Skyscrapers: I love New York.

MYTH ALERT

However, two strange myths relate to Wingdings, the graphical font that pre-dates Wingdings. One is that if you type NYC in Wingdings you get:

supposedly an anti-Semitic message. The other is that if you type Q33NY in Wingdings you get:

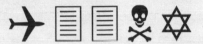

According to a bizarre conspiracy theory, Q33NY was the tail number of one of the 9/11 planes and this proves that 9/11 was targeted at New York Jews. Of course, it wasn't the tail or flight number of any plane involved and 9/11 was indiscriminate in its targeting of any specific religion.

35. IN THE PAPER

CARTOON STRIPS

Some long-running newspaper comic strips only make sense if you are a regular reader. To everyone else it's like Tolstoy publishing *War and Peace* one line at a time, for a century!

■ **DOONESBURY** Garry Trudeau's comic strip has run since 1970. Syndicated all over the world, *Doonesbury* has a large cast of fictional characters.

Trudeau likes to include real people in his strip, mainly from politics, depicted as icons or symbols. Each symbol is a satirical take on an aspect of their personality. For example:

ROMAN HELMET OVER AN ASTERISK	George W. Bush. Originally a Stetson over an asterisk, Bush's foreign policy led Trudeau to replace it with an 'imperialist' Roman helmet, which has become increasingly battered
GIANT GROPING HAND	Governor Schwarzenegger
LARGE WAFFLE	Bill Clinton, for a tendency or be indecisive
UNEXPLODED CARTOON BOMB	Newt Gingrich
INVISIBLE MAN	George Bush senior
QUAIL FEATHER	Dan Quayle, former Vice President
SWASTIKA	David Duke, white supremacist

■ **DILBERT** Dilbert the luckless office cubicle dweller is the creation of cartoonist Scott Adams. Dilbert is usually drawn with his tie upturned, however Adams told (only) the recipients of his newsletter that if Dilbert ever 'got lucky' with love interest Liz, he'd draw his tie flat. This finally happened on 9.8.94.

■ **GARFIELD** On 1 July 1st 2007 the *Garfield* strip was secretly dedicated to illustrator Jim Davis' first assistant and sole inker for many years, Valette Green, who died in January 2007. Davis changed the usual logo to feature Garfield's eyes being inked in. On the last panel, you can just see 'Valette' picked out in stars.

■ **'MATT'** The *Daily Telegraph*'s pocket cartoonist 'Matt' (Pritchett) said on a recent *Desert Island Discs* that he tries to include his wife somewhere in his cartoons. Matt once committed the sin of drawing a Royal Navy officer with a moustache. Naval officers may sport either a 'full set' (moustache and beard) or nothing.

■ **AL HIRSCHFELD** The American caricaturist (1903–2003) hid the name of his daughter Nina in his drawings (the number after his signature tells you how many to look for).

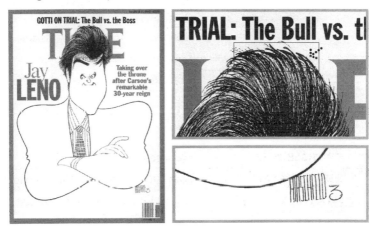

Hirschfeld also included caricatures of himself and wife Dolly in drawings with crowds of people. Hirschfeld is a bearded gentleman, Dolly is a thin woman with large black dots for eyes and a black dot for a mouth, creating a bowling-ball looking face. Hirschfeld drew satirical portraits of stars from Chaplin to the cast of *Star Trek TNG*. He drew some of the original posters for *The Wizard of Oz* (1939). Much to his disgust, the U.S. Army used his 'Ninas' to train bomber pilots to spot targets. In 1991 he drew a series of postage stamps of famous American comedians. The U.S. postal service broke a rule and allowed him to include Ninas in his drawings.

(*See* 21. **IN THE POST**; 4. **IN CLOTHES**, '*Spy v Spy*' *Trainers*)

CRYPTIC CROSSWORDS

The relationship between compiler and solver is a cat-and-mouse game reminiscent of Hannibal Lecter and Clarice Starling.

Broadsheet compilers often use pseudonyms. 'Torquemada' and 'Ximenes' reflect the nature of their work: both were torturers in the Spanish Inquisition. Crossword compilers exchange thumb-screws and presses for anagrams and homophones. *Times 2* crossword compiler John Grimshaw once designed a puzzle where two rows of letters consisted entirely of 'O's and 'I's, spelling out the number of that crossword (3903) – in binary.

Confused, mixed up, wild, replaced etc.	Anagram: reordering letters of a word to make new word, e.g. DESIGN and SINGED
Cut short	Take letters off the end of a word, e.g. 'Realtor' becomes REAL
Initially	First letter only of each word in clue, e.g. 'Initially crook rakes in many euros doing what?' CRIME
Involved in	Answer hidden between two words, e.g. 'Skins mango for uncle' contains the word KINSMAN

Late	'd' for dead
North, South, East, West	Cardinal letters N, S, E and W
Notes	Often a musical note, ABCDEFG
Pole(s)	N or S, or the first and last letters of a vertical word
Scotsman	Often 'Ian' at the end of word, e.g. COMEDIAN
Son or daughter	Stands for letters S or D
Upset, mounted, rising etc.	Often in a 'Down' clue, which should be read from the bottom up
We hear, they say, sounds like etc.	Homophone: word that sounds the same but is spelt differently e.g. TAUT and TAUGHT
Without	In the sense of 'outside', e.g. in the word SAINT the word SAT is 'outside' the word 'IN'

TABLOID CODE

If someone dies, the tabloids indicate their worth by words like 'father-of-three', 'mum', 'loner' or 'graduate'. An 18-year-old male is a 'teenager' if he is a victim but a 'man' if he is the perpetrator.

AXE	Cancel	**DEATH PLUNGE**	Fall
BLAST, SLAM	Criticise	**FUME**	Get annoyed
BOFFIN	Scientist	**GONG**	MBE
BRAVE	Terminal cancer	**GRANNY**	Woman over 40
CAGED	In prison	**KO'ED**	Knocked out, fired from job
CLASH	Disagree		
CLOSE FRIEND	Any source	**KOP**	Liverpool

LAG	Convicted prisoner	**POSH**		Posh Spice, i.e.
MUM	Nice woman			Victoria Beckham
NEIGHBOUR	Anyone living in a	**QUIZ**		Question
	10 mile radius	**ROMP**		Sex
PENSIONER	Any woman over	**SWOOP**		Raid
	60, man over 65	**TOFF**		Posher than you
PLUCKY, TRAGIC	With a disability			

OBITUARY COLUMN CODE

When Hugh Massingberd (1946–2007) joined the *Daily Telegraph*, he turned obituary writing from the brackish backwater of journalism into an art form, using what the *New York Times* called 'cataclysmic understatement and carefully coded euphemism'. For example, in this *Daily Telegraph* obituary from 1991:

> *The Third Lord Moynihan, who has died in Manila, aged 55, provided through his character and career ample ammunition for critics of the hereditary principle*

As well as 'bon mots', obit writers have unsystematically developed words and phrases that regular readers can decode.

■ OBITUARY COLUMN CODE

After a short illness	**Possibly suicide**
Complications from pneumonia	**Possibly AIDS**
Convivial, rubicund	**Drunk**
Did not suffer fools gladly	**Miserable bugger who hated everyone**
Died suddenly	**Probably suicide**
Fastidious, confirmed bachelor	**Gay**

Fun-loving, flirtatious, loveable rogue	**Serial skirt-chaser**
Gave colourful accounts of his exploits	**Liar**
Long-term companion/friend	**Gay partner**
Man of simple tastes	**Common**
Never afraid to say what she thought	**Unspeakably rude**
Never at a loss for words	**Never shut up**
No discernible enthusiasm for human rights	**Closet Nazi**
One of a kind	**Thank God**
Plain-speaking	**Rude**
Powerful negotiator	**Bully**
Relished physical contact	**Sadist**
Strongly held beliefs	**He's right, you're wrong**
Tireless raconteur	**Tiresome bore**
Uncompromisingly direct ladies' man	**Flasher**
Vivacious	**Tart**

LONELY HEARTS CODE

By charging by the word (30 max), newspapers encourage lonely-hearts to use acronyms or code-words to communicate with each other.

You probably know 'N/S' (non-smoker), 'GSOH' (good sense of humour, and 'WLTM' (would like to meet). In the 21st century things are more complicated…

DDF	Drug/disease free
FTM	Female to male transgendered (and MTF)
HWP	Height-weight proportional

MBA	Married but available – explains the statistic that 35% of people using personal ads for dating are already married
NBM	Never been married
OHAC	Own house and car
S/A	Straight-acting (gay not camp)
SPARK	Single parent raising kids
TDY	Temporarily divorced yesterday
BIG HUGS	Romance, no sex
CUDDLY, CHUNKY, VOLUPTUOUS	Fat
GREAT TEETH	Just don't look at the rest of me
PETITE, KYLIE LOOKALIKE	Short
SEEKS LADY TO SPOIL	Will pay for sex
SEEKS WHITE MALE	Racist
SNUGGLES, FUN, FRIENDSHIP – POSSIBLY MORE	Wants sex
STRAWBERRY	Ginger hair
YOUNG 47	Over 50
420 FRIENDLY	Dope fiend

■ **BLUEBEARD** (see opposite) From 1914 to 1919, with WW1 creating a surplus of widows, Henri Landru placed adverts in the lonely hearts columns of Parisian newspapers:

Widower with two children, aged 43, with comfortable income, serious and moving in good society, desires to meet widow with a view to matrimony.

MLLE. MARCHADIER

MME. JAUME

MLLE. BABELAY

MME. COLOMB

MME. CRUCHET

LANDRU'S

GARDEN

MME. LABORDE LINE

MME. GUILLIN

MME. BUISSON

MME. PASCAL

BLUEBEARD.

Nice, except that Landru was 'Bluebeard', one of France's worst serial killers. Landru protested his innocence and no bodies were ever found. Nevertheless he was guillotined in 1922 for murdering eleven women. Before he died, Landru gave his lawyer a drawing he made in prison. The lawyer hung it in his office. Over forty years later, the lawyer's daughter found a message on the back of the drawing: 'I did it. I burned their bodies in the kitchen stove.'

Landru inspired Chaplin's *Monsieur Verdoux* (1947) and appeared as a character in the Doctor Strange stories in Marvel comics.

ESCORT AGENCIES

While we're on the subject, escort agencies use code to advertise their services to those in-the-know. Here are some of the less graphic (seriously): *overleaf.*

A LEVELS	Anal sex
BBW	Big beautiful woman
BJ	Blowjob
CAT BATH	Lick all over
CD	Cross dressing
CDS	Covered doggy-style (with condom)
CIM	Come in mouth
CMD	Carpet matches drapes e.g. natural blonde
CP	Corporal punishment
DP	Double penetration
FS	Full sex
GFE	Girlfriend experience
HR	Hand relief
MÀF	Woman who was a man
FÀM	Man who was a woman
MFS	Massage, full sex
O LEVELS	Oral Sex
OTK	Over the knee (spanking)
OWO	Oral (sex) without (a condom)

PSE	Porn star experience
RR	Rough rider
SWO	Sex without (condom)
TG	Transgender
TLC	Tender loving care
TV	Transvestite
W/S	Watersports

CODED MESSAGES

During the Cold War the CIA and FBI used the *New York Times* personal columns to communicate with Soviet informant Dmitri Polyakov:

> **Moody, Donald F,** please write as promised. Uncle Charles and Sister Clara are well and would like to hear from you. Don't forgot address, Dave, Doug and spouses. Travelling? When, where? We hope for family reunion soon. Regards and best wishes, brother Edward H and John F close to New Jersey.

'Donald F' is Polyakov. 'Edward F' is Edward Moody, Polyakov's case officer. 'John F' is John Mabey, Moody's boss. 'Sister Clara' is the drop site where Polyakov left and received messages. If there was a problem he should use another drop site, 'Dave' or 'Doug'. 'Travelling?' meant is Polyakov leaving the USSR soon, if so Mabey would organise a 'family reunion' or meeting. Polyakov was betrayed by CIA double agent Aldrich Ames.

(*See also* 13. **IN ESPIONAGE,** *Chalk Marks*)

In March 1966 the World Cup was stolen from the Central Hall in Westminster and held to ransom by a man calling himself Jackson. In the ransom note Jackson demanded £15,000 saying: 'To me it is only so much scrap gold. If I don't hear from you by Thursday or Friday at the latest I assume it's one for the POT'.

As instructed, Joe Mears, Chairman of the FA, replied via the 'Personals' column of London's *Evening News*:

Willing to do business Joe

Jackson, real name Edward Betchley, was arrested by police, but claimed he was only the middleman. The Cup was eventually found by accident under a hedge by a dog called Pickles (left).

CODED MESSAGES

In 2000, an Enigma code machine was stolen from Bletchley Park. It was returned anonymously to journalist Jeremy Paxman but three vital rotors were missing. The *Sunday Times* negotiated secretly for the rotors' return via codewords placed in the 'Personals' column of *The Times*.

THANKS SAINT JUDE

Many people put a message in the Personals thanking St. Jude, patron saint of desperate situations, for answering their prayers. For centuries, Jude was the forgotten saint, because Christians identified him (wrongly) with Judas Iscariot, the disciple who betrayed Jesus.

WORK FROM HOME!

Look out for the secret signs. If the advert…

- asks for money
- has a free hotmail account to reply to
- is hosted on a free site like Tripod or Angelfire
- doesn't mention the nature of the job
- asks you to add your name to a list
- guarantees income but requires no skills or previous experience

…then it's a scam.

MAGAZINES

Next time you're at the dentist's or hairdresser's try this entertaining secret sign to work out which gender has been reading which magazines.

Apparently women read magazines forwards, first page to last, so the pages curl *towards* the reader. Men tend to read a newspaper backwards, beginning with the sports pages at the end. As a result they usually read magazines backwards too, making the pages curl *away* from the reader.

36. ON A CAR

NUMBER PLATES

Registration plates stir up great emotion. Beijing motorists were furious that the 2007 plates included 'WC', an abbreviation of Water Closet even in China. The authorities won't change it, despite a precedent: in Xinyang, Henan Province, the letters 'SB' were removed as they are used in chat rooms to represent the Mandarin phrase shǎbī = stupid person (lit. 'stupid c**t').

In car commercials, number plates may be designed to be read in a mirror. For example, 818 ATA reads ATA 818 when reversed. That way still or moving images can be 'flipped' to create left- or right-handed vehicles, depending on where the car is being marketed.

PERSONALISED NUMBER PLATES

The desire to possess personalised plates is as old as plates themselves. In 1903 Earl Russell, brother of philosopher Bertrand, queued all night to obtain the very first UK plate: A1, for his Napier.

The Queen's personal plate, A7, was issued in 1907. The 'A' stands for London. For official business the Queen has no number plate. The only other person in the UK with this privilege is the Lord High Commissioner to the General Assembly of the Church of Scotland, and then only for the week of the annual Assembly.

In the US, some letter combinations are reserved for movies, such as RUM and URN. In 2008 the most expensive plate to date was bought for $14.2 million by Abu Dhabi businessman Saed Abdul Ghaffar Al-Khouri at an auction. In the UAE, the shorter your number plate, the higher your status. Mr. Al-Khouri's new plate is simply '1'. (*See more on HM Queen's car in* 30. **AT THE PALACE**)

I DLT	ex-Radio 1 DJ Dave Lee Travis
I KO, IIIKO	Chris Eubank
I TEL	Terry Venables
2BE, NOT 2B	Pair of cars in a private garage in Chelsea
5I NGH	Sold in 2006 for £254,000 to a Sikh buyer. 'Singh' is Punjabi for 'lion' – symbol of bravery. Guru Gobind Singh gave every Sikh male the same name to remove the discrimination of the Indian caste system
AMS I	Sir Alan 'You're Fired' Sugar, from *The Apprentice*
BI7CH X	Women's boxing champ Cathy Brown
CHU8B	Chris Tarrant (for Chubb, his favourite freshwater fish)
CIGAR	Cigar importers Hunters & Frankau (on their van)
COMIC	Jimmy Tarbuck, comedian
DS 500	Lord (David) Steel, Lib Dem peer
H4I RDO	Nicky Clarke (i.e. hairdo)
MAG IC	Paul Daniels, magician
MI	Mike McCoomb, former owner of the Mobile Phone Store, bought for £331,500 in 2000. Apparently he bought it for his eleven-year-old son
MR DIY	*Ground Force* builder Tommy Walsh (Mr. D-I-Y)
ORV IL	Keith Harris, after his puppet Orville
RA I	Richard 'Dickie' Attenborough, film director and peer
S8 RRY	Robbie Williams as an apology to fans for spending so much on a Ferrari. In the end, he opted for a moped

TIP ME	London taxi
T8	Johnny Tate, of Tate & Lyle (*See also* 41. **FOOD**, *Golden Syrup*)
VIP I	Roman Abramovich, Chelsea FC owner. Previously on John Paul II's Popemobile when he visited Ireland

In the U.S. you might see the license plate TI-3VOM. If the car comes up behind you, you'll see MOVE-IT in your mirror!

HOW TO READ A UK NUMBER-PLATE

In the current system (since 2001) the first two letters identify the area. The middle two numbers represent the year of manufacture. The final three letters are random. Consider the two letters. The first identifies the region (e.g. A for Anglia). The second tells you in which DVLA office the car was registered.

REGION		DVLA OFFICE	
(EAST)	A	Peterborough	A – N
ANGLIA		Norwich	O – U
		Ipswich	V – Y
BIRMINGHAM	B	Birmingham	A – Y
CYMRU/WALES	C	Cardiff	A – O
		Swansea	P – V
		Bangor	WXY
DEESIDE ETC.	D	Chester	A – K
		Shrewsbury	L – Y
ESSEX AND HERTFORDSHIRE	E	Chelmsford	A – Y
FOREST AND FENS	F	Nottingham	A – P
		Lincoln	R – Y
GARDEN OF ENGLAND	G	Maidstone	A – O
		Brighton	P – Y

HAMPSHIRE AND DORSET	H	Bournemouth	A – J
		Portsmouth	K – Y
		Isle of Wight	HW
KETTERING AND LUTON	K	Luton	A – L
		Northampton	M – Y
LONDON	L	Wimbledon	A – J
		Stanmore	K – T
		Sidcup	U – Y
MANCHESTER & MERSEYSIDE	M	Manchester	A – Y
NORTH	N	Newcastle upon Tyne	A – O
		Stockton-on-Tees	P – Y
OXFORD	O	Oxford	A – Y
PRESTON AND PENNINES	P	Preston	A – T
		Carlisle	U – Y
READING	R	Reading	A – Y
SCOTLAND	S	Glasgow	A – J
		Edinburgh	K – O
		Dundee	P – T
		Aberdeen	UVW
		Inverness	X/Y
SCOTLAND (ADDITIONAL)	T	Glasgow	TF07 only
		Edinburgh	TK07, TN07 only
VALE OF SEVERN	V	Worcester	A – Y
WEST COUNTRY	W	Exeter	A – J
		Truro	K/L
		Bristol	M – Y
YORKSHIRE	Y	Leeds	A – K
		Sheffield	L – U
		Beverley	V – Y

Now look at the two numbers. The first tells you whether the car was made in March or September. The second number tells you which year, so for example '53' means September 2003.

YEAR	MARCH	SEPT	YEAR	MARCH	SEPT
2001	—	51	2002	02	52
2003	03	53	2004	04	54
2005	05	55	2006	06	56
2007	07	57	2008	08	58
2009	09	59	2010	10	60
2011	11	61	2012	12	62
2013	13	63	2014	14	64
2015	15	65	2016	16	66
2017	17	67	2018	18	68
2019	19	69	2020	20	70

DIPLOMATIC PLATES

Diplomatic plates follow the formula of three letters, one letter, three numbers. The first group of numbers identifies a country or organisation. The middle letter is either 'D' for diplomats (embassies or consulates) or 'X' for non-diplomatic staff. The second group of numbers is a serial number.

101	AFGHANISTAN	102	ALGERIA
103	ARGENTINA	104–108	AUSTRALIA
109	AUSTRIA	110	BAHAMAS
111	BAHRAIN	112	BANGLADESH
113	BARBADOS	114	BELGIUM
115	BENIN	116	BOLIVIA
117	BOTSWANA	118–122	BRAZIL

123	BULGARIA	124	MYANMAR
125	BURUNDI	126	CAMEROON
127–131	CANADA	132	CENTRAL AFRICAN REP
133	CHAD	134	CHILE
135	CHINA	136	COLOMBIA
137	CONGO	138	COSTA RICA
139	CUBA	140	CYPRUS
141	CZECH REPUBLIC	142	DENMARK
143	DOMINICAN REPUBLIC	144	ECUADOR
145–147	EGYPT	148	EL SALVADOR
149	ETHIOPIA	150	FIJI
151	FINLAND	152–156	FRANCE
157	GABON	158	GAMBIA
159 163	GERMANY	164	FORMER GDR
165	GHANA	166–167	GREECE
168	GRENADA	169	GUINEA
170	GUYANA	171	HAITI
172	HONDURAS	173	HUNGARY
174	ICELAND	175–179	INDIA
180	INDONESIA	181–182	IRAN
183–184	IRAQ	185	IRELAND
186–187	ISRAEL	188–190	ITALY
191	CÔTE D'IVOIRE	192	JAMAICA
193	JAPAN	194–195	JORDAN
196	KENYA	197	KOREA
198	KUWAIT	199	LAOS
200	LEBANON	201	LESOTHO
202	LIBERIA	203	LIBYA

204	LUXEMBOURG	205	MALAWI
206	MALAYSIA	207	MALI
208	MALTA	209	MAURITANIA
210	MAURITIUS	211	MEXICO
212	MONGOLIA	213	MOROCCO
214	NEPAL	215–217	NETHERLANDS
218–219	NEW ZEALAND	220	NICARAGUA
221	NIGER	222–224	NIGERIA
225	NORWAY	226	OMAN
227–228	PAKISTAN	229	PANAMA
230	PAPUA NEW GUINEA	231	PARAGUAY
232	PERU	233	PHILIPPINES
234	POLAND	235	PORTUGAL
236	QATAR	237	ROMANIA
238	RWANDA	239–240	SAUDI ARABIA
241	SENEGAL	242	SEYCHELLES
243	SIERRA LEONE	244	SINGAPORE
245	SOMALIA	246–247	SOUTH AFRICA
248–252	RUSSIAN FEDERATION	253–255	SPAIN
256	SRI LANKA	257	SUDAN
258	SWAZILAND	259	SWEDEN
260	SWITZERLAND	261	SYRIA
262	TANZANIA	263	THAILAND
264	TOGO	265	TONGA
266	TRINIDAD	267	TUNISIA
268	TURKEY	269	UAE
270–274	USA	275	URUGUAY
276	VENEZUELA	277	VIETNAM

278-279	YEMEN		280	YUGOSLAVIA
281	DR CONGO		282	ZAMBIA
283	DOMINICA		284	MONACO
285	NAURU		286	ST LUCIA
287	UGANDA		288	BURKINA FASO
289	ST VINCENT		290	ZIMBABWE
291	VATICAN		292	EAST CARIBBEAN
293	BELIZE		294	BRUNEI
295	ANTIGUA		296	ANGOLA
297	GUATEMALA		298	MOZAMBIQUE
299	NAMIBIA		300	LITHUANIA
301	ARMENIA		302	SLOVENIA
303	LATVIA		304	ESTONIA
305	CROATIA		306	UKRAINE
307	SLOVAKIA		309	ALBANIA
312	BOSNIA		315	KAZAKHSTAN
316	GEORGIA			
350-400	MAY BE USED BY ANY EMBASSY FOR SECURITY REASONS			
600-650	MAY BE USED BY VISITING ROYALTY ON OFFICIAL VEHICLES			

■ INTERNATIONAL ORGANISATIONS

900	Commonwealth Secretariat
901	Commission for the European Community
902	Council of Europe
903	European Centre for Medium-Range Weather Forecasts
904	European Organisation for Safety of Air Navigation
905	European Parliament
906	Inter-American Development Bank

907	International Maritime Organisation
908	International Cocoa Organisation
909	International Coffee Organisation
910	International Finance Corporation
911	International Labour Organisation
912	International Sugar Organisation
913	International Tin Council
914	International Whaling Commission
915	International Wheat Council
916	North Atlantic Treaty Organisation
917	United Nations
918	Western European Union
919	World Health Organization
920	Eastern Caribbean Commission
921	Joint European Torus
922	International Oil Pollution Compensation Fund
923	International Maritime Satellite Organisation
924	Commonwealth Foundation
925	International Maritime Organisation (Permanent Representative)
926	Commonwealth Telecommunications Bureau
927	United Nations High Commissioner for Refugees
928	Commonwealth Agricultural Bureau
929	International Lead and Zinc Corporation
930	Oslo and Paris Commissions
931	Joint European Torus
932	North Atlantic Salmon Conservancy Organisation
933	European Investment Bank

934	European Telecommunications Satellite Organisation
935	European School (Oxford)
936	African Development Bank
937	European Bank for Reconstruction and Development
938	European Bank for Reconstruction and Development
940	European Bioinformatics Institute
941	European Medicines Agency

In London red police cars belong to the DPG (Diplomatic Protection Group)

ACCESSORIES

■ **DOG STICKER** Dogging enthusiast. Not to be confused with nodding dogs on the back shelf: that would mean everyone's at it! (*See also* 29. **IN THE COUNTRY,** *Dogging*)

■ **BLUE GARTER** Brides traditionally wear 'something blue' on The Big Day such as blue garters. The groom removes one and throws it into the crowd like the bridal bouquet (the guy who catches it is the next to be married). Some brides keep the other garter and hang it from their rear-view mirror as a symbol of lurv. Ever so slightly kinky. (*See also* 26. **AT A CHURCH WEDDING,** *Something Borrowed*)

■ **ROSARY** Roman Catholic. The Virgin Mary is often represented in art as a walled rose garden or 'rosary' – a symbol of her womb and perpetual virginity, after the Song of Solomon (4:12) in which the beloved is referred to as 'a garden enclosed, a fountain sealed up'. (*See also* 19. **IN ART,** *Art Symbols*)

■ **STYLISED FISH** Christian, probably not Catholic. The Romans persecuted early Christians for their faith. Worn

as a badge or marked on a wall the fish symbol became a secret means of recognition, along with the anchor, trident and axe. (*See* 25. **IN CHURCH**, 27. **IN A CHURCHYARD**).

■ **TASSEL** US students wear mortar boards with a tassel at their graduation ceremony. The tassel is worn to the right before graduating, to the left shortly after. Graduates often hang their tassels from their rear-view mirror. Tassels may come with charms showing the year they graduated, and in different colours according to the degree:

PE	Sage Green	EDUCATION	Light Blue
NURSING	Apricot	SCIENCE	Golden Yellow
MUSIC	Pink	JOURNALISM	Crimson
ECONOMICS	Copper	ENGINEERING	Orange
FINE ARTS	Brown	LIBERAL ARTS	White
MEDICINE	Kelly Green	VET MEDICINE	Grey
THEOLOGY	Scarlet	LAW	Purple

■ **FUZZY DICE** A pair of dice in your motor still says 'boy racer'. But retro is chic and dice have become a 'girlie' accessory, as likely to be seen in a brand-new Mini Cooper.

In the 1950s a pair of dice were a good-luck charm, carried in your pocket and later hung from the rear-view.

They may originate even earlier, in 1930s America during the Prohibition, as a symbol of Speakeasy gambling.

In *Star Wars* (1977) see if you can spot a pair of metallic dice hanging in the cockpit of the Millennium Falcon (in later shots they disappear), possibly referring to the fuzzy dice in Harrison Ford's car in George Lucas's *American Graffiti* (1973).

■ **THE SMELLY TREE** The pine-scented evergreen tree is often found on the rear views of smokers or dog owners (trying to hide the smell).

Tree deodorants hang in every car in *Repo Man* (1984) – including the police motorcycle.

MYTH ALERT

There are many urban legends surrounding the Crown air-freshener. It is owned by the KKK. It is the badge of a particular gang, or a Black separatist, or a high-up in the drug world. Nope, it's just a plastic crown.

Another myth says that a CD dangling from your rear-view mirror will bamboozle a police radar or speed-camera by reflecting the flash backwards, either obscuring your number plate or confusing the radar. Similar principles have led drivers to coat their plates in hairspray and even cover their wheels in tinfoil.

None of these methods work (honestly) but CDs continue to dangle, often as a decorative accessory or religious item. Some contain copies of the Koran.

■ **CHILD ON BOARD** The yellow diamond-shaped sign has cutesified into 'Pampered Princess', 'Little Twin Stars', even 'Child of God on Board'.

However it is not, as many new parents think, a twenty-first-century fertility symbol. Yellow diamond signs mean 'warning'. This one warns the emergency services attending a car crash to look for a small body.

■ **OM** A major Hindu symbol, OM is the primordial sound, the first breath of creation, the vibration that ensures existence. OM signifies God and the Oneness of creation.

■ **ST CHRISTOPHER MEDAL** St Christopher is the patron saint of travellers. 'Christopher' literally means 'carrying Christ'. Hanging his medal from your mirror is a token to prevent accidents. In *Life on Mars*, Sam Tyler wears a St. Christopher medal to represent his journey through time (or to keep him safe in Gene Hunt's Cortina!)

(*See also* 25. **IN CHURCH**; 18. **ON TELEVISION**, *Life on Mars* and *Ugly Betty and Anne Boleyn*)

EMERGENCY LIGHTS

As well as the obvious (police, fire, ambulance), blue lights can be used by the MoD (bomb disposal), the Forestry Commission (forest fires), vehicles carrying blood for transfusion or transplant tissue, the Coastguard, British Coal Corporation (mine rescue), and Revenue & Customs. Green indicates a doctor's car, amber is for breakdown trucks, bin lorries etc. Red flashing lights are totally forbidden.

UNMARKED POLICE CAR

How to spot a 'bear in a plain wrapper':

- Two people in front seats
- Two rear-view mirrors
- Very clean and well-maintained
- No dealer's sticker in rear window, no salesroom ad on numberplate
- Empty parcel shelf, except for occasionally a long flat box (in fact a sign that lights up)
- Alloy wheels, no hub caps, to aid driving if the tyres are blown out
- Engine sounds more powerful than the car model
- Preferred models include: Citroen AX, Ford Galaxy, Ford Mondeo, Saab 95, Vectra V6, Vauxhall Omega V6

MYTH ALERT

If you're driving in the dark and you see a car driving with its headlights off, don't flash your lights: the driver is undergoing a gang initiation, and must kill the first person to flash a warning.

This urban legend has been around for over twenty years. The warning is 'issued' by different emergency services and relates to different gangs (e.g. Bloods, *See* I. **MEETING**). Like the best urban myths, it sounds plausible and can be adapted to suit any place or time. And like the best myths, it isn't true!

A less sinister myth is that the 'petrol pump' icon on your dashboard tells you which side of the car your fuel tank is on. If the pump handle is on the left, so is your tank. If only it were that simple!

LOGO AREA

We take vehicle logos for granted. Their effect is so governed by advertising we lose sight of their original meanings. Some are personal: the Lamborghini bull reflects the birth sign of its creator (Taurus). The initials JCB belong to the mechanical digger and its creator, John Charles Bamford. Here are some more.

BMW

According to legend, the BMW logo represents an aeroplane propeller. According to BMW this is a myth, stemming from a 1929 advertisement which used the roundel in rotating propellers to help increase sales of their radial aircraft engines for Pratt & Whitney. However, the blue and white quadrants are the colours of Bavaria (BMW stands for Bayerische Motoren Werke or Bavarian Motor Works.)

MERCEDES-BENZ

The Mercedes-Benz logo is not a propeller either! It is simply a star in a circle.

Founder Gottlieb Daimler once worked at the Deutz gas engine factory. In 1872, he sent a picture postcard of Cologne and Deutz to his wife. He marked a star above his own house and wrote that this star would shine over his own factory one day. Gottlieb's sons Paul and Adolf remembered the star and incorporated it into the Mercedes logo.

MITSUBISHI

Means 'three diamonds' in Japanese, which its logo represents.

AT THE PETROL STATION

■ **BP** In 1923, the French operation of BP added the colours green and yellow to the old BP shield. According to BP the palette was inspired by thoughts of nature and spring. According to legend it was inspired by an asparagus-and-Chablis lunch enjoyed in Paris by senior management.

■ **SHELL** Ultimately from the scallop shell worn by pilgrims on their way to the shrine of St James at Santiago de Compostela in Spain.
(*See* 2. **ACCESSORIES**, *Scallop Shell* for more).

■ **Q8** Kuwait Oil Company – based on the English pronunciation of 'Kuwait', and the twin sails of a traditional Kuwaiti sailing ship.

MORSE ALERT

In a Honda, if you leave the keys in the ignition or the headlights on, the warning tone is [---], H for Honda.

37. ON A MOTORBIKE

With limited visibility and hearing, bulky gloves and a desire to stay upright on two wheels at speed, motorcyclists have their own hand signals, especially when riding in a group. Look out for:

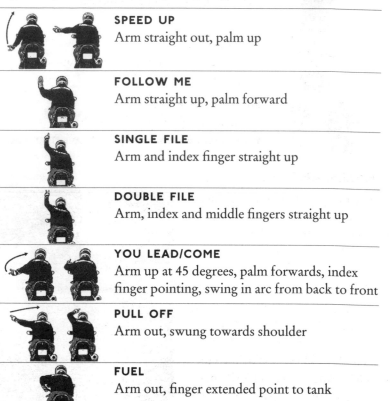

SPEED UP
Arm straight out, palm up

FOLLOW ME
Arm straight up, palm forward

SINGLE FILE
Arm and index finger straight up

DOUBLE FILE
Arm, index and middle fingers straight up

YOU LEAD/COME
Arm up at 45 degrees, palm forwards, index finger pointing, swing in arc from back to front

PULL OFF
Arm out, swung towards shoulder

FUEL
Arm out, finger extended point to tank

BEAMS ON
Tap top of helmet, open palm down
Also sometimes 'Warning, police ahead'

TURN SIGNAL ON
Open and close hand
Also sometimes 'You've left your signal on'
(Bike indicators have no automatic cancel)

REFRESHMENT STOP
Fingers closed, thumb to mouth

COMFORT STOP
Arm out, fist clenched, short up-and-down
motion

HAZARD IN ROAD
Point with right or left foot or hand
Foot extended is sometimes 'Thank You'

HELLS ANGELS

The first sign a rider is a member of the Hell's Angel Motorcycle Club is the bike, a Harley-Davidson.

The Hells Angels name was reputedly suggested to an Angels founder by Arvid Olsen, a member of the 303rd Bombardment Group, a WW2 unit of the USAF, nicknamed the 'Hell's Angels'. The HAMC has no apostrophe, apparently because there is 'more than one hell'.

On the jacket, you will find a Death's Head insignia (which the HAMC have trademarked!) said to originate from insignia designs of the 85th Fighter Squadron and the 552nd Medium Bomber Squadron.

Also on the jacket, look for number 81, substitution code for HA (eighth and first letters of the alphabet). The official colours of the Angels are red and white. Angels have a system of patches, indicating for example whether or not they are full members, which chapter they belong to, what rank they hold etc.

The red-and-white '1%' patch is a joke and a badge of honour. In 1947, the American Motorcyclist Association responded to the behaviour of an earlier motorcycle fraternity, the elegantly named 'Pissed Off Bastards', by saying that 99% of motorcyclists were law-abiding citizens, and the last 1% were 'outlaws'. The Angels like to associate themselves with that 1%.

MOVIE ALERT

In the movie *Alfie* (2004), Jude Law's Vespa is blue and white as a tribute to the team he supports, Spurs.

38. ON A LORRY

TRUCKER TO TRUCKER

When one lorry passes another, the slower driver flashes his lights to say: 'You've passed me now, it's safe to go back into the inside lane'. At night, drivers flash their lights off-and-on instead to avoid blinding the other driver.

To say: 'Thanks for letting me out', they may flash their indicators one way, then the other. Flashing your lights to another driver while pointing your thumb down apparently means 'warning, speed trap ahead'.

LORRY LINGO

To earn your Yorkie-bar badge study the following list. A 'tractor unit' is the section of a lorry doing the pulling i.e. the cab, the 'trailer' is whatever the tractor's pulling:

BANKSMAN	Anyone who helps a driver reverse
BARN DOORS	Big doors at the back of the trailer
BEAVER TAIL	Fold-up ramps for driving vehicles on and off a flatbed
COW BELL	Lead carrying current from tractor unit to trailer
FIFTH WHEEL	U-shaped plate on the back of a tractor unit on which the trailer swivels
MOFFAT (BRAND)	Forklift truck that piggybacks on the back of a trailer
RUNNING BENT	Driving when you've run out of driving hours
RUNNING BOBTAIL	Driving a cab without a trailer

SUZIES	Leads from tractor to trailer sending electricity to the lights, and air to the brakes and suspension
TAUTLINER	Trailer with taut plastic sides that fold back like a curtain
TRAMPING	Living and sleeping in your lorry while you are working

CB SLANG

Citizen's Band slang has declined since C.W. McCall sang 'Mercy sakes alive, looks like we got ourselves a convoy!' due to mobile phones and satellite radio. But if you're trying to decode a Burt Reynolds movie, here's a handy list:

BACKSIDE/FLIP-FLOP	Return trip e.g. 'See you on the backside'
BEAR/SMOKEY	Cop: in a **PLAIN WRAPPER** (unmarked car), with **EARS** (listening to CB) in a **BEAR DEN** (police station)
BONE BOX	Ambulance
BUSTER BROWN	UPS lorry
CHICKEN LIGHTS	Every extra light on a rig
CHOKE 'N' PUKE	Restaurant
DISCO LIGHTS	Flashing lights on a police car
EARS	CB radio (as in 'you got your ears on?')
EIGHTY-EIGHTS	Love and kisses (from Morse code slang)
EVIL KNIEVEL	Bear on a motorbike
FRONT DOOR	Leader of a convoy
HAMMER LANE	Fast lane
HOW MANY CANDLES YOU BURNING?	How old are you?

KICK A TIRE/10-100	Have a pee
KITTY LITTER	Salting the road
KOJAK WITH A KODAK	Bear with a radar gun or speed camera
LOT LIZARD / SLEEPER LEAPER	Prostitute
MISS PIGGY	Female police officer
MOTION LOTION	Fuel
ORGAN DONOR	Motorcyclist
PARKING LOT	Stationary traffic
PICKLE PARK	Rest area frequented by lot lizards
PREGNANT ROLLER-SKATE	VW Beetle

Hitler inspects a
'pregnant rollerskate'

ROACH COACH	Mobile café
SIN CITY	Vegas
SHAKY TOWN	Los Angeles
SKATEBOARD	Flatbed truck or trailer
SUICIDE JOCKEY	Driver hauling explosives
TWENTY	Location ('What's your twenty?') from 10-20

39. IN AN EMERGENCY

POLICE SCANNER CODES

American police codes vary from area to area, so the following selection is a guide only. It does however give a telling insight into the life of a US police officer.

10-00	OFFICER DOWN	10-1	POOR RECEPTION
10-3	STOP TRANSMITTING	10-4	MESSAGE RECEIVED
10-9	REPEAT LAST MESSAGE	10-10	FIGHT IN PROGRESS
10-12	STANDBY	10-14	SUSPICIOUS PERSON /PROWLER
10-15	CIVIL DISTURBANCE	10-16	DOMESTIC DISTURBANCE
10-20	SPECIFY LOCATION	10-23	ON LOCATION
10-24	EMERGENCY BACKUP	10-26	DETAINING SUSPECT
10-27	DRIVERS LICENCE CHECK	10-28	VEHICLE REGISTRATION CHECK
10-29	ARRESTS/WARRANTS CHECK	10-31	CRIME IN PROGRESS
10-32	PERSON WITH GUN	10-33	EMERGENCY, ALL UNITS STAND BY
10-34	RIOT	10-35	MAJOR CRIME ALERT
10-37	SUSPICIOUS VEHICLE	10-40	RUN SILENT
10-45	ANIMAL CARCASS	10-52	AMBULANCE NEEDED
10-54	NEGATIVE	10-55	DRUNK DRIVER
10-57	HIT AND RUN	10-66	OFFICER WELLBEING CHECK
10-70	FIRE ALARM	10-77	ETA
10-78	NEED ASSISTANCE	10-80	PURSUIT IN PROGRESS
10-87	PRISONER TRANSFER	10-89	BOMB THREAT
10-90	ALARM GOING OFF (E.G. BANK)	10-91	PICK UP PRISONER/SUSPECT
10-94	STREET RACING	10-95	PRISONER/SUSPECT IN CUSTODY
10-98	ASSIGNMENT COMPLETE/ JAILBREAK	10-99	CARDIAC ARREST/DEATH

10-105	DOA	10-108	OFFICER DOWN
10-109	SUICIDE		

'INSPECTOR SANDS' AND FRIENDS

You hear regular announcements on the London Underground asking 'Inspector Sands' to attend a particular location. This means a fire alarm has been activated at that location. It does not necessarily mean a fire has actually broken out. If you're subsequently told to leave, start worrying. If you hear that Inspector Sands (like Elvis) 'has left the building', you can stop worrying.

The name originated in theatres, where 'Mr Sands' was a fire alert code, referring to the old-fashioned sand bucket used for extinguishing fires.

'Mr Sands' is still used in theatres, restaurants, sports ground, concert arenas etc. Chelsea supporters may hear 'Mr Bridge' after their home ground of Stamford Bridge. 'Mr Ash' is sometimes used for a fire alert, and

'Mr Case' for a suspect package. A passenger under a tube train is called 'one under' or a 'brown liner'. If you are on an ocean liner, listen out for 'Phoenix' (code for fire) and 'Niagara' (work it out).

On the 1997 PopMart tour, U2 arrived in a giant lemon spaceship, from which the band emerged surrounded by dry ice and smoke. If the spaceship door got stuck, which was often, the emergency code 'Lemon failure' would go out across the PA system.

SKYJACK

Back in the 1970s, the biggest terrorist threat was having your airliner hijacked and flown to Tripoli. Aircraft were equipped with transponders, radio transmitters that send out automatic signals. The emergency frequency was 3100: if an aircraft squawked on 3100, it was assumed it had been hijacked.

SWAT TEAM SIGNALS

In emergency situations, SWAT (Special Weapons and Tactics) and other rapid-response teams use hand signals to minimise noise.

| ONE | TWO | THREE | FOUR | FIVE | SIX | SEVEN | EIGHT | NINE | TEN |

YOU	ME	COME	LISTEN OR I HEAR
WATCH OR I SEE	HURRY UP	STOP	FREEZE
COVER THIS AREA	I UNDERSTAND	I DON'T UNDERSTAND	HOSTAGE

SNIPER

OBSTACLE

CELL LEADER

COLUMN FORMATION

FILE FORMATION

ENEMY

WEDGE FORMATION

RALLY POINT

PISTOL

RIFLE

SHOTGUN

AMMUNITION

VEHICLE

DOOR

WINDOW

POINT OF ENTRY

GO HERE OR
MOVE UP

LINE ABREAST
FORMATION

CROUCH OR GO
PRONE

40. IN HOSPITAL

TAKING THE MICKEY

In 2007 a hospital in Burton-on-Trent got into trouble for using Winnie-the-Pooh as a secret sign. Pharmacy staff at the Queen's Hospital used a picture of the little bear on the doors of their out-of-hours drugs store. Only they knew that Pooh was an acronym of 'Pharmacy Out Of Hours'.

Drugs in hospitals can attract unwanted attention, so it could be seen as a responsible move. Sadly Disney were not amused by the connection between their copyright image and drugs.

MEDICAL NOTES

GPs and hospital doctors are famous for writing notes only FBI graphologists can read and reducing complex living beings to acronyms. And like funeral directors and traffic cops, their gallows humour helps create a necessary distance between the professional and the personal. What other profession could come up with the 'MacTilt' – the caring tilt of the head of a palliative-care specialist (after Macmillan Nurses)?

■ WHAT THEY THINK ABOUT YOU:

FATHER JACK	Elderly confused male patient, usually shouting random offensive words (after character in *Father Ted*)
GANFYD	Get A Note From Your Doctor: patient who's just come in to get a note, whatever they say
GLM FLK	Good-Looking Mum, Funny-Looking Kid
GROLIES	Guardian Reader Of Low Intelligence In Ethnic Skirt
NFN	Normal For Norfolk

NPS	New Parent Syndrome (also DPS, Dumb Parent Syndrome)
PUMPKIN POSITIVE	If you were to shine a penlight into the patient's mouth, his whole head would light up (due to lack of a brain)
SIG	Stroppy Ignorant Girl
TMB	Too Many Birthdays

■ THE DIAGNOSIS:

AWTB	Away With The Birds
TEETH	Tried Everything Else, Try Homeopathy
LOLNAD	Little Old Lady, No Apparent Distress (also 'Handbag Positive')
HIBGIA	Had It Before, Got It Again
WNL	Within Normal Limits OR We Never Looked
PAN	Pissed As a Newt
PFO	Pissed and Fell Over
FTF	Failed To Fly (of attempted suicide)
GOK	God Only Knows
UBI	Unexplained Beer Injury
DISCO BISCUITS	Ecstasy
TTFO	Told To F**k Off. Asked by a judge to explain this on a patient's notes, a doctor came up with 'To Take Fluids Orally'!
HEARTSINK	Patient whose arrival makes your heart sink

■ THEY THINK IT'S ALL OVER:

| CTD | Circling The Drain. 'Chasing Zebras, Circling The Drain' was the working title of US medical drama *House* |

TBUNDY	Totally F**ked But Unfortunately Not Dead Yet
GPO	Good for Parts Only
BTBLO	Box To Bedside, Lid Open

■ PARAMEDICS

Paramedics are often first on the scene, particularly to road traffic accidents. As a result they have developed a series of acronyms that are 'close to the bone' (hehe). These are from American paramedic crews. You have been warned.

CATS	Cut All To Shit
CC	Cancel Christmas
DND	Damn Near Dead
FDSTW	Found Dead, Stayed That Way
MARWB	Met At Road With Bag
PBS	Pretty Bad Shape
PEFYC	Pre-extricated For Your Convenience (through the windscreen)
TBC	Total Body Crunch
WUD	Woke Up Dead

■ HOSPITAL SLANG

ASH CASH	Money received for completing cremation forms
COLD TEA SIGN	Number of cups of cold tea around the bedside indicate that the patient died a while ago but no one noticed
DEPARTURE LOUNGE	Geriatric ward
DIGGING FOR WORMS	Varicose vein surgery

DIRT BAG INDEX	Multiply number of missing teeth by number of tattoos to work out number of days since the patient last washed
ETERNAL CARE	Intensive Care Unit
FREUD SQUAD	Hospital psychologists
GASSERS & SLASHERS	Anaesthetists and General Surgeons
HOUSE RED	Blood
KNIFE & GUN CLUB	Inner City Hospital

OVER THE TANNOY

Hospital emergency codes vary from region to region and country to country. Here is a flavour.

■ CODE

BLUE	Medical emergency, patient near death
RED	Smoke or fire (usually followed by location)
PINK	Child abduction (also 'Adam')
BROWN	Faeces-related emergency
GREEN	Vomit-related emergency
ORANGE	Hazardous materials spill
PURPLE	Prepare for evacuation

■ PAGING DOCTOR

STRONG	Fight breaking out (also Mr Speed)
PURPLE	Chemical spill
POWER	Electricity problem (e.g. power cut)
STORK	Obstetrics emergency
ABLE	General major incident, help needed
RED	Fire alert

In TV and movie hospital scenes, paging fictitious doctors over the tannoy is a regular in-joke.

■ PAGING

DR SANDY ZOBER
In *Star Trek IV: The Voyage Home* (1986). Sandra Zober was then Leonard Nimoy's wife

DR HOWARD, DR FINE, DR HOWARD
In *Inspector Gadget* (1999). Moe Howard, Larry Fine, and Shemp Howard were the Three Stooges!

DR BENWAY
In *Repo Man* (1984), based on William Burroughs' short story. Dr Benway is a character in Burroughs' *The Naked Lunch*

DR KRIPKE
In *Supernatural* (TV) Season 2:1. Reference to series' creator and executive producer, Eric Kripke

STABLE...

When dealing with the media, many hospitals have a policy of referring to a patient's condition only as follows:

- SATISFACTORY
- IMPROVING
- STABLE
- SERIOUS
- CRITICAL

FAKING IT

If you're pretty sure someone is just pretending to be asleep, try this neat nurses' trick. Pick up their hand, hold it high above their forehead – and let go. If they smack themselves, they're out for the count. If they stop the drop, they're faking.

41. IN FOOD & DRINK

SWISS BEAR

The familiar logo of Swiss chocolate Toblerone is the Matterhorn mountain. But do you see the 'hidden' silhouette of a bear on its hind legs, formed by the snow on the mountain? Like the Fedex arrow, this is a 'bonus' graphic. If you don't see it, you don't miss it, but if you do you get a warm fuzzy feeling. The bear is the symbol of Bern, capital of Switzerland.

(*See also* 21. **IN THE POST**, *Logo Area*)

MARGHERITA PIZZA

The popular pizza is designed to resemble the flag of Italy: red tomatoes, green basil and white mozzarella cheese. It was made by Neapolitan chef Raffaele Esposito in 1889 for the Italian Queen, Margherita.

KFC

In 2006, KFC built an 87,500 square foot Colonel Sanders logo and hid a secret message in it for a competition. The giant logo was visible from space, and was photographed by the GeoEye satellite from 423 miles uphigh. To add to the mystery, the logo was built in the Area 51 desert in Nevada, beloved of UFOlogists. The message was 'finger lickin' good'.

IN-N-OUT BURGERS

Visit Arizona, Nevada or California, and you may come across this family-owned hamburger chain, founded in 1948. What you may not notice are tiny notations on various cups and wrappers, listing verse numbers of passages from the Bible.

For example, the hamburger and cheese wrappers bear the message 'Revelation 3:20', the milkshake cup 'Proverbs 3:5', and the soda cup John '3:16':

For God so loved the world, that He gave His only Son, that whosoever believeth in Him shall not perish, but have everlasting life.

(*See also* 15. **IN SPORT**, *The Rainbow Man for more on John 3:16*)

GOLDEN SYRUP

If you think the British wouldn't do this, look at a tin of Tate & Lyle's Golden Syrup. The logo is a dead lion surrounded by a swarm of bees. The words come from Judges 14, reflecting Abram Lyle's strong religious faith. On the way to the land of the Philistines, Samson kills a lion. On the way back, he sees that bees have formed a honeycomb in the lion's carcass. He turns this into a riddle:

Out of the eater came forth meat and out of the strong came forth sweetness.

HEINZ 57 VARIETIES

'57' has never been the number of Heinz products. It was chosen by Henry Heinz as an advertising gimmick (5 and 7 being psychologically favourable numbers), inspired by an ad for '21 styles of shoe' that Heinz saw on a billboard.

Heinz also make Alphabetti Spaghetti. There is a bizarre internet rumour that during WW2, a special version of the tinned food was made in Germany in the shape of swastikas. You couldn't make it up, but someone did.

PINEAPPLES

The pineapple is a traditional symbol of welcome, as the centrepiece of a table display or carved in wood or stone.

(*See also* 11. **ON A BUILDING**)

MINCE PIES

The Crusaders brought many influences back from the Holy Land, including spices. Mince pies originally contained meat and shredded suet, mixed with dry fruit and three spices – cinnamon, cloves and nutmeg – representing the three gifts of gold, frankincense and myrrh brought to the baby Jesus by the Wise Men. Apparently the pies were once made in tins shaped like cradles to represent the manger. During the Commonwealth, Oliver Cromwell banned them!

CROISSANTS

There are a number of stories about the origins of this pastry. In one version, probably mythical, the croissant (French for 'Crescent') was invented by Viennese bakers in 1683 to celebrate surviving an attack by the Ottoman Turks. They were designed to represent a flag of Turkey you could eat!

CHINESE MOON CAKES

According to legend, these delicacies were secretly used to start a revolution by the Chinese against the Yuan (Mongol) dynasty in the fourteenth century.

Moon cakes are pale round cakes made of flour and filled with a variety of fillings. During the Moon festival they are traditionally made by women at home and distributed to friends and family.

The story goes that in the fourteenth century, messages calling for coordinated insurrection were baked into moon cakes during the Festival and sent to thousands of people, right under the noses of the rulers. The resulting uprising led to the overthrow of the Yuan dynasty and the beginning of the Ming dynasty.

SECRET SIGNS OF WINE

A thousand years of wine appreciation cannot be reduced to a few paragraphs. But let's give it a go.

Tilt your glass wine and a few streaks of colourless liquid will be left on the inside of your glass. These are the 'tears' or 'legs' of the wine, consisting mostly of alcohol. The more viscous the tears, the higher the percentage of alcohol in the wine. To judge the age of a white wine – the paler it is, the older it is. For a red wine, look at the meniscus: the outer edge of the liquid where it meets the glass. If the colour is paler around the meniscus, it is an older wine.

BISHOP OF NORWICH

When passing the Port, if someone asks you 'Do you know the Bishop of Norwich', it isn't a social inquiry. The Bishop was famously stingy, so the phrase means you're keeping the decanter too long, preventing anyone down the line from getting it.

FINISHED

If you haven't finished your meal, don't rest your cutlery on the plate. To signal that you have finished, put your knife and fork together with the handles pointing towards 5 o'clock (the 'correct' position varies in different part of Europe).

NAPKINS

If you have to leave the dinner table temporarily, put your napkin on your chair. This is a signal that you will be back. When you leave the table for good, lay it unfolded beside your plate.
NB: this doesn't work in restaurants.

DINER SLANG

This secret language used by short-order chefs and restaurant staff in the U.S. is full of humour and wit, even if some of the shorthand is longer than the original!

Adam and Eve on a raft	Two poached eggs on toast
Bailed Hay	Shredded Wheat
Bow-wow, Bun Pup	Hot dog
Cow Feed	Salad
Dough well done with cow to cover	Buttered toast
First Lady	Spare ribs (from Eve)
Frog Sticks	French Fries
Hockey Puck	Hamburger, well done
Honeymoon salad	Lettuce alone (let us alone)
Lighthouse	Bottle of ketchup
M.D.	Dr. Pepper
Million on a platter	Baked beans
Murphy	Potato
Noah's boy	Slice of Ham (one of Noah's sons)
On a rail	Fast!
Pigs in a blanket	Ham sandwich
Pin a rose on it	Add onion
Smear	Margarine
Walk a cow through the garden	Hamburger with lettuce, tomato and onion

(*See also* 16. **IN A NUMBER**, *86 and 68*)

CELEBRITY PSEUDONYMS FOR BOOKING RESTAURANTS OR HOTELS

Brian Bigbun	**ELTON JOHN** (also Bobo Latrine)
Thomas Paine	**VAL KILMER**, after eighteenth-century pamphleteer
Jacques Strap	**HUEY LEWIS**
Stanley Kowalski	**JON BON JOVI**, after a character in *A Streetcar Named Desire*, played by Marlon Brando
Harry Bollocks	**OZZY OSBOURNE**
Miss Orange	**DIANA ROSS**
Bella	**BRITNEY SPEARS**
B. Simpson	**TIGER WOODS**, after Bart Simpson
Carl Con Carne	**BRAD PITT**
Sir William Marshall	**MICHAEL JACKSON**, after an English knight
Sigourney Beaver	**KATE BECKINSALE**
J.C. Penney	**BONO**, after the American department store
Mr. Satan, Mr. Donkey Penis	**JOHNNY DEPP**
Miss Lollypop	**ANGELINA JOLIE**
Mrs. Smith	**JENNIFER ANISTON**
Arnold Schwarzenegger	**GEORGE CLOONEY**

42. AT THE BINGO

Bingo calling is becoming a thing of the past, as modern clubs want quicker games, and technology allows everyone to see and hear the numbers being called.

1	**KELLY'S EYE**	Australian gangster Ned Kelly had one eye
8	**ONE FAT LADY**	Shape
9	**DOCTOR'S ORDERS**	In WW2 army medics had a pill drawer with compartments for different medicines. Pill no. 9 was a laxative
10	**GORDON'S DEN**	Downing Street, changed for each PM
12	**MONKEY'S COUSIN**	Rhyme
16	**NEVER BEEN KISSED**	Sweet Sixteen
21	**KEY OF THE DOOR**	Coming of age

23	**THE LORD'S MY SHEPHERD**	Psalm 23
26	**BED & BREAKFAST**	2s 6d, traditional cost of a night's lodging
27	**DUCK AND A CRUTCH**	2 looks like a duck, 7 like a crutch
30	**BURLINGTON BERTIE**	Tic-Tac slang for 100-30
33	**SHERWOOD FOREST**	Lots of trees (threes)
39	**THOSE FAMOUS STEPS**	John Buchan book
49	**PC 49**	1940s-50s radio show
50	**BULL'S EYE**	Darts score
80	**GANDHI'S BREAKFAST**	Probably homophone 'Ate nothing'
83	**FAT LADY WITH A FLEA**	8 resembles fat lady, 3 rhymes with flea

(*See* 15. **IN SPORT**, *Tic-Tac*. 33. **OVERHEARD**, *Rhyming Slang*)

43. IN PARLIAMENT

PARLIAMENTARY CODE

Members of the Houses of Commons and Lords use traditional coded phrases that baffle the public they serve. As well as leaving to 'spend more time with my family' (i.e., forced to resign), here are more official phrases:

Another place	The House of Lords if you're in the Commons, and vice versa
Chiltern Hundreds Manor of Northstead	MPs can't resign voluntarily during a Parliament, so they must accept an 'office of profit' under the Crown (legally disqualifying them from continuing as an MP), either the Manor of Northstead or the Chiltern Hundreds, both within the gift of the Chancellor of the Exchequer

Hear, Hear	Applause is not customary in the House (except on rare occasions such as Tony Blair's farewell PMQ)
Honourable and gallant	The MP is or was in the Forces
Honourable and learned member / friend	The MP referred to is a practising lawyer
I Spy Strangers!	The coded request for members of the public to leave the Commons galleries was abolished in 1998, along with many other traditions. For example, if a member wished to raise a point of order during a division, they would stay seated but put on a collapsible opera hat kept by the Sergeant-at-Arms.
My honourable friend	Member of your own party
St. Thomas's	Members may not die on the premises as Westminster is a Royal Palace (and commoners may not die in a palace). Any death is said to have taken place at St. Thomas', the nearest hospital.
The member opposite, or the honourable member	Member of the Opposition (in parliament, Government and Opposition sit opposite each other)
Who goes home?	Shouted by Palace of Westminster police at the end of each day's sitting

ACKNOWLEDGEMENTS

I would like to thank: my editors Ben and Jack at Hodder & Stoughton for their guidance, wisdom and support; my agent Zoë King at Darley Anderson for believing in me and in this book from the very start – her enthusiasm is infectious; Tony Lyons, for the book's superb design; Eric and Carole Massey, whose beautiful garden in Brittany gave me the inspiration to get started; Roy Ackerman at Diverse Production for loaning me an office before the walls of my study began to close in; Betty Mason for information (and photography) about the Croix de Lorraine; Alan Rose of the Inn Sign Society; and David G. Croft and Adrian Pegg for their knowledge of album covers and motorbikes respectively.

I'd like to extend a special thank you to David Bodycombe, friend and fellow author, who has given me many ideas and leads for *Tic-Tac* and kept my chin up when it has started to sag.

Finally, thanks and apologies to the two women in my life, for putting up with me during the writing of this book – and the rest of the time too. Love love.

PICTURE ACKNOWLEDGEMENTS

Alamy: 13 (© Homer Sykes), 43 (Joe Sohm), 49 left (© Andrea Heselton), 62 left (Travelshots.com), 63 (© Regis Martin), 73 (© Genevieve Vallee), 156 (© Stan Pritchard), 165 (© Paul Salmon), 171 (© Adrian Muttitt), 174 (© Kevin Britland), 175 (© Dave Porter), 176 (© Andrew Holt), 224 (© Corbis Premium RF), 226 (© VStock). Bridgeman Art Library: 119, (Phillips Auctioneers UK), 135 below (Private Collection), 169 (Private Collection). Craig Burgess: 32, 62 right, 82 below left and right. The College of Arms, London: 179. Corbis: 18, 42, 129 below, 133, 137, 228, 229, 237. Jim Fitzpatrick: 124. Getty Images: 8, 11, 12, 14, 17, 19 above, 21, 23 above and below, 25, 28, 29, 31, 34, 37, 38, 40, 60, 66, 70 above, 71, 72, 78, 80, 82 above, 87, 94, 96, 97, 99, 100, 101, 104, 105, 110, 114, 116, 128, 129 above, 138, 142, 153, 154, 164, 167 right, 177, 190, 191, 203, 209, 212, 214, 231, 232, 235, 247. istock: 251, 253, 256.Linns.com: 130. MOD Crown Copyright: 77 centre. National Gallery, London: 24, 121, 123. National Maritime Museum: 193. National Portrait Gallery, London: 57 left, 146. Nonstock: 33. PA Photos: 90, 93. Westminster Abbey, The Library: 26. Brett Woods: 76 below. Zimpenfish: 61.

Most other images courtesy the author.

Every reasonable effort has been made to contact the copyright holders, but if there are any errors or omissions, Hodder & Stoughton will be pleased to insert the appropriate acknowledgement in any subsequent printing of this

Private!